RELEASE
TO
RECEIVE

by
JONATHAN W. ALLEN, SR.

E xulon
LITE

This book is dedicated to my
anointed and amazing wife for life,
Kimberly Yvette Reeder Allen.
Thank you for loving me, praying for me
and supporting me beyond measure!

Acknowledgments

I am thankful to God for the message of deliverance that He has led me to articulate in this literary work, which will help many to release that which binds them and receive all that awaits them.

To my wonderful wife, Kimberly R. Allen, who is my biggest supporter in life and who consistently supports me through prayer and encouragement!

To my son, Jonathan W. Allen, Jr., and my grandson, Jaquan J. McShay, who constantly push me to think outside of the box with their innovative young minds!

To our team of professionals, who spent hours to help this vision become a reality:

Thank you Dr. Larry Keefauver (Powerhouse Families), Dr. Izola Jones (Professional Christian Counseling), Renee McMullen (MTM Consulting, Marketing/Events), and Janine Coveney (Syllable Media, LLC, Editorial Services).

To all others who participated in reviewing this manuscript, thank you.

Table of Contents

Foreword

Still Learning the Secret of *Release To Receive*
By Dr. Larry Keefauver

W hat a joy it has been for me to encourage Pastor Allen in the development and writing of this tremendous teaching treatise. Years ago, I had the privilege to work with Bishop T.D. Jakes and Dr. Jack Hayford who teamed with me to edit *Ministries Today* magazine. Jakes' book *Woman Thou Art Loosed: Healing the Wounds of the Past* started an important movement in the biblical teachings around "releasing and receiving." Dr. Hayford's writing on deliverance through cleansing streams also opened the church up to dimensions of the truths in this book. The Faith Movement with Kenneth Hagin and Kenneth Copeland gave us powerful teachings on how to declare by faith God's promises to receive the abundant life Jesus promises us in John 10:10. Jonathan Allen, Sr., now steps into this teaching and ministry flow with this important contribution, *Release To Receive.*

His life is an exciting testimony for Christian Families, Church Ministers, Christian Professionals, and Kingdom Business Leaders on how to be loosed, released, and set free from hindrances, bondages, past failures, and personal failures and sin, so that believers in all walks of life can receive the wonderful blessings of God through Christ Jesus.

The principles of *Release To Receive* are powerfully taught in the pages of this book. Inspiring and biblically solid, these spiritual keys have unlocked for me insights and practical spiritual disciplines for experiencing the new season God has for each of us as our old, fruitless seasons come to a close.

Every believer can profit from learning the secrets to Kingdom business and living in this book. The declarations, prayers, and 30-day spiritual journal at the end of the book are a priceless treasure for releasing the old and receiving all the new things God has for His children. As a pastor and pastoral counselor, I have learned so much I will be sharing with those that I coach and counsel with in ministry and business.

I want to thank Pastor Allen for sharing with me the original message he preached on Hannah's petitions for a child in the Presence of God. Her releasing paved the way for her to receive the blessing of Samuel. Furthermore, in releasing her tears, she received overflowing joy. This message as it is developed in *Release To Receive* has impacted my life for following Christ in new and refreshing ways. It will do the same for you.

Treat your spirit to a fresh drink of wisdom, knowledge, and understanding from the river of the Holy Spirit. Take a short, personal retreat from the cares of this world to read this book from beginning to end. Walk through the 30-day declaration journal at the end. Discover for yourself the mighty power God has given to you in being able to *Release to Receive.*

-Dr. Larry Keefauver
Bestselling Christian Author and International Teacher
Maui, 2016

Introduction

See, I am doing a new thing!
Now it springs up; do you not perceive it?
- God speaking through an ancient prophet to *you!*

The message I am sharing with you is for us—you and me. All of us have issues. I know that I have challenges in my personal life, in ministry, at work, and in my relationships. As with storage units—many people keep their past stuff locked up and out of sight. They pay a periodic rental charge to hold on to old furniture, clothes, household goods, tools, and the overflow of stuff that they feel they must keep. If you have a storage unit, and you are never using or going to use most if not all of the stuff you keep there, why are you holding on to it? It's costly and probably unnecessary.

Years ago, a short play depicted a prisoner sitting dejectedly in a jail cell. For years he had been wasting away in his small, damp, terrible room passing his days in lonely depression. He never talked with those who brought him his food passed through an opening in his door. He refused to leave the cell for meals, exercise, or any other activity.

One day, a stranger opened the door and announced good news, "You've been set free. You have been released."

Walking away, the stranger left the door open with the keys still hanging from the door's lock. Shaking his head in disbelief, the inmate walked over to the cell's door, shut it, reached through the food opening in the door, took hold of the keys, relocked the door, and tossed the keys out of reach. He returned to his lonely stool and continued on with his daily habits—unchanged, hopeless, and still imprisoned ... by his own choice. Does this story sound like anyone you know? Does it tell your story?

Are we locked up and imprisoned by our past? Some of us have stored up *stuff* from early childhood, through our teenage years, and into adulthood. It's called baggage. We hold on tightly to past disappointments, failures, abuses, hurts, pain, and failures. We choose to be imprisoned by the past instead of releasing it and going forward. Instead of *Failing Forward,* as author John C. Maxwell advises us to do in his 2000 bestseller, we fail backward, languishing in the mire and pits of our past junk. Like people who hold on to storage units and stuff they don't need and may never use, we hoard former negative thoughts, beliefs, feelings, behaviors and attitudes for years—and for those who are older than 20, for decades. Reality shows on television depict "hoarders," "pickers," and "storage wars." Many of us do the same things internally that the stars of these shows do externally.

When is the right time to start releasing our baggage, throwing out unneeded and unnecessary stuff, and walk out of the prison cell of our past? When will we start listening to and obeying God when He counsels us:

Forget the former things;
do not dwell on the past.

See, I am doing a new thing!
Now it springs up; do you not perceive it?
I am making a way in the desert
and streams in the wasteland.
(Isaiah 43:18-19 NIV)

We've got to *release* some stuff in order for us to be able to *receive* what God has in store for us individually as well as collectively.

The word *"release"* means:

- *to be set free from restraints and confinements*
- *to let go of what's holding us back, slowing us down, burdensome*
- *to move from one's normal, static, and staid position to a new place, posture, and plan*

Have the nightmares of your past taken your present captive robbing you of your rest, renewal, and refreshing in God's new thing? Holding on to the past costs a lot of time, money, and energy. Think about those storage units for a moment. Each month one pays a rental fee—sometimes in the hundreds of dollars. All the while, the stuff being stored continues to age, rust, mildew, and collect mold. Insects and bacteria eat away at its worth. Jesus speaks passionately about this: "Do not lay up for yourselves treasures on earth, where moth and rust destroy and where thieves break in and steal; but lay up for yourselves treasures in heaven, where neither moth nor rust destroys and where thieves do not break in and steal. For where your treasure is, there your heart will be also" (Matthew 6:19-21 NKJV).

❧

**Whatever you refuse to release,
restricts your progress and retards your growth.
When will you release what holds you back, so you can
receive the new thing God has for your future?**

❧

The word *"receive"* means:
- *to acquire and accept*
- *to come into possession of*
- *to grasp and take hold of*
- *to permit something new and different to enter into our lives*

We must release the baggage, the past, the stuff and junk of the former things in order to receive the treasures, gifts, and opportunities of the new things from God. The old "normal" must pass away; the new "normal" must come. The good and bad ideas of the past have run their course; God and fresh plans for the present and future must begin to bloom in the desert. In the Book of Isaiah, God promises to make a way through and out of the desert and the dry place. He pledges to bring us out of the lonely, isolated and thirsty expanses of life where we get stuck, locked in, chained, and sorely habitual about. These are places where we can develop negative feelings, depressing thoughts, unconstructive and destructive behaviors, along with seemingly endless cycles of failed plans, disappointing relationships, and unproductive, unfruitful work. We stay busy but never seem to be creative, fruitful, and prosperous.

Are you ready to release your issues and baggage, unlock and empty out the storage bins of your life, and leave the wilderness where you've been circling but never getting anywhere? Jesus promises release for the captives, water for the thirsty, bread for the hungry, and hope for the hopeless. Take a moment. Check off √ which of the following things you need to release or baggage you need to let go of:
- Failed relationship with a spouse, parent, child, or relative
- Loss of a job, career, or business
- Miscarriage or inability to conceive
- Financial loss, foreclosure, or bankruptcy
- Being abused, misused, manipulated, dominated, or intimidated
- Flunking out of a course, a certification, a promotion, or new career track
- Not finishing an important project or completing a plan

- Forgetting to keep a promise, engagement, appointment, or meeting

Now check off what you hope to **receive**:
- A fresh start, a new beginning.
- Forgiveness from a person you have hurt
- Restoration of a relationship
- New dreams, visions, plans and purpose

In this book, you will be invited to release the past and receive the new things God has for your present and future. I will share with you the ancient story of a woman named Hannah, who learned much from God about releasing and receiving. What I received from her story not only instructed and inspired me, I was changed and impacted forever. You will be, too. Come with me as you release the old and receive the new!

Chapter 1

Creatures of Habit

Now there was a certain man from Ramathaim-Zophim from the hill country of Ephraim, and his name was Elkanah the son of Jeroham, the son of Elihu, the son of Tohu, the son of Zuph, an Ephraimite. He had two wives: the name of one was Hannah and the name of the other Peninnah; and Peninnah had children, but Hannah had no children. Now this man would go up from his city yearly to worship and to sacrifice to the Lord of hosts in Shiloh. And the two sons of Eli, Hophni and Phinehas, were priests to the Lord there. When the day came that Elkanah sacrificed, he would give portions to Peninnah his wife and to all her sons and her daughters; but to Hannah he would give a double portion, for he loved Hannah, but the Lord had closed her womb. Her rival, however, would provoke her bitterly to irritate her, because the Lord had closed her womb. It happened year after year, as often as she went up to the house of the Lord, she would provoke her; so she wept and would not eat. (1 Samuel 1:1-7)

The Lord has allowed me to make this statement several times and that is: *We are creatures of habit.*

Some of us do the same thing, the same way, day after day, month after month, year after year. Some of us come in and won't even change our praise. We won't even change our worship because we are creatures of habit. There was a sermon the Lord allowed me to preach years ago, "When Wrong Seems Right." We've been doing wrong for so long that it actually seems right. You've been treating your husband or your wife mean for years and you've been doing it for so long you think it's right. It's wrong! You've been smoking for so long that it becomes a norm and you think it is right, but you're killing the temple of your body and it's wrong. You have been watching the wrong thing on the computer or television for so long that it now seems acceptable; you've been using profane language so long that it sounds OK to you now.

୶

When what's wrong has become so habitual it seems right; then your habitual sin will lead you down the path of destruction blinding you to warning, remorse, and repentance.

୶

Even our right habits can become so ritualistic that we go through the motions without ever engaging our hearts, never feeling the need to change and become the person Christ wants us to be. Scripture reminds us that the person who knows what is right to do and doesn't do it, has committed a sin.

We are creatures of habit, yet that's not a bad thing if the habit is habitual righteousness and not habitual sin. If the habit is rooted in that attitude, spoken and done with the right motive, then the right outcome will happen. This is so important: The right words and actions, done in the right way, at the right time for the right reasons produce right outcomes—allowing us to release past baggage and receive present and future blessings. We will see how all of this works for Hannah.

❧

**Right words and actions,
done in the right way,
at the right time,
for the right reasons,
produce right outcomes,
putting us in the right place...
to *release* past baggage,
and *receive* present and future blessings.**

❧

Bring Your Problems to the Problem Solver

In 1 Samuel 1, we read that there was a man named Elkanah from the hillside of Ephraim and Elkanah had two wives. Certainly, he must have had issues—and lots of baggage. Monogamy is a blessing but it can be challenging at times; I cannot imagine the issues and baggage that polygamy can create for its practitioners. Yet we read that this man had two wives, one named Hannah and the other, Peninnah. Peninnah had children, but Hannah did not. In ancient Hebrew culture, women were valued and seen as blessed when they had children. However, being barren was often seen as a curse and a woman without a child was scorned.

We often place value upon ourselves and others based on productivity. After all, didn't God create us according to Genesis 1:22 to be fruitful and multiply? So ancient Semitic tradition valued a man by what his work produced and a woman by what her womb produced. Today many still place a high value on being able to have children. Therefore we can certainly empathize and understand why the barren Hannah went to the temple, prayed to God, and wept.

As creatures of habit, Elkanah and his family would go up to Shiloh every year to worship, and make sacrifices unto the Lord.

When he would make the sacrifices, he would give a portion of the meat to Peninnah, his wife, and to her sons, and he would give to her daughters. Then the Scripture says he would give a double portion to his wife, Hannah, "because he loved her." When you love somebody you don't mind giving them a double portion.

Hannah had received this double portion from Elkanah, but one thing that she did not receive was the ability to give birth to children. The Scripture says that the Lord had shut up her womb. The Scripture goes on to tell us that this was an embarrassing condition for Hannah. Childlessness was a circumstance that grieved Hannah day in and day out.

Some of us, even in our present situations, exist with conditions that are truly embarrassing. Our issues, past baggage, and former desert seasons in life have created some conditions that can truly grieve our spirits when we begin to focus on them. Some of us have situations so critical that we are forced to confront because they grieve us, day in and day out. This applies not only to grown men or women, but to boys and girls as well. The great news is that we can come to a place where we can release these things in order to receive what God has in store for us. But it should be the right place, in the right time.

Get to the Right Place to Find Release

As Hebrew worshippers, Elkanah and his wives habitually took their sacrifices to the tabernacle at Shiloh. To paraphrase a current Geico insurance commercial, if you're an ancient Hebrew family, you go to Shiloh to make sacrifices to God—it's what you do. They were doing the right thing, at the right time, for the right reason—worshipping the Living God of Abraham, Isaac, and Jacob.

Don't make light of the fact that you habitually go to worship and focus on God. His presence is the right place and worship is the right time to bring your issues to God. When you go to the place of release, take the problem to God the problem solver. Hannah went to the right place, at the time as prescribed by the Torah, the Hebrew Law, and did the right thing.

The scriptural narrative tells us that Peninnah provoked Hannah, talked about her, gave her a hard time, aggravated her, and irritated her about her condition. We all know some people like that, some folks who will irritate you, some folks who will aggravate you, some folks who will annoy you just because you don't have what they have. So the story goes on to tell us that yearly Elkanah went up with both wives and family in order to worship. And Peninnah would constantly just badger Hannah, talk about her, and give her a hard time. Scripture says that when they went up to worship, she would constantly get on Hannah's nerves.

It got to a point that Hannah began to weep sorely. Hannah was crying and could not even eat, so Elkanah went to her and said, "Why are you crying, why are you going through all that you're going through?" When she explained, Elkanah replied that he loved her more than he could possibly love ten sons. Now any man knows when you have one son, you're mighty proud of that one son. There are some folks who have only had girls and are still trying to have boys, because it's a man thing. He loved her more than ten sons. That's an overflowing, abundant, double portion love.

So, let's pause here to examine some important spiritual steps about release for these Hebrew creatures of habit who did the right things.

1. *The Right Place* – Do the right things in God's way. The right place to get to the root of your past and present issues is in God's presence as you worship and pray. The wrong place is to blame others or fight with them. Certainly Hannah could have gone to her husband to try to solve her problems. Her husband actually did the wrong thing to try to fix the problem. His love for his wife prompted him to give her more thus trying to compensate for her lack. Wrong thing even if his motives were right. Doing the wrong thing, at the wrong time, even with the right motives will only increase the problems. No human can fix our past problems. Hannah kept her focus right, i.e. righteous. She took her problems to God.

2. *The Right Way* – Refuse to be caught up in sinful, human habits that blame others for your feelings, thoughts, and behaviors. Hannah did not complain to her husband or fight with the wife who was taunting her. Instead, because she was in God's presence, in the right place at the right time, she chose the right way to release her past.

Let me help you out here. Sometimes, we need to avoid or eliminate the wrong ways to handle the past before we can act upon release in the right way. Here's a list of the wrong ways, i.e. the bad and sinful habits we revert to when we are hurting, distressed, and struggling through our deserts in life:

- Blaming others
- Complaining
- Fighting
- Feeling angry and depressed
- Making others look bad believing we will look and feel better
- Becoming a victim
- Eating
- Shopping
- Being a workaholic

3. *The Right Time* – Worship and prayer are always the right time when we are in God's place and presence to release past baggage, issues, and problems. Everyone loves a Three-Step Solution and the Scriptures provide us one here:

- **Repent** – Turn away from the bad habit, the past problem, the habitual sin and turn toward the Problem Solver, God in Christ Jesus.
- **Release** – Let go of it. Evangelist Dr. Larry Lea used to say, "Admit it; Quit it; and Forget it." We will discuss this more in future chapters. Admittedly, forgetting it isn't easy.
- **Receive** – Let God give you His blessing, in His way, and in His timing.

Yes, Hannah brought quite a lot of baggage to the tabernacle at Shiloh. Her suitcases were full of disappointment, regret, pain, hurt, accusations, and attacks. She could have reverted to sinful human habits and kept all her pain inside. As we say, she could have chosen to put on her "church face" or masked her real feelings so she would appear to the priests and her family to be happy, content, and satisfied with life.

But she didn't deny, repress, or regress. Her past did not determine her present or shape her future. In the right place—in God's presence, in the right way—releasing to God her problems without being trapped by a multitude of negative feelings, thoughts and actions, and at the right time—in worship and prayer—Hannah found release and was able to *stand up* and go forward into God's future for her.

Let's now turn to how she *stood up released, walked about from her past, and received hope and blessing from God.*

> "Let go of the past so that God can open the door to your future."
>
> ~Author Unknown~

Chapter 2

Time to Stand Up

So Hannah rose up after they had eaten in Shiloh, and after they had drunk. Now Eli the priest was sitting upon his seat by the door-post of the temple of Jehovah. And she was in bitterness of soul, and prayed unto Jehovah, and wept sore. And she vowed a vow, and said, O Jehovah of hosts, if thou wilt indeed look on the affliction of thy handmaid, and remember me, and not forget thy handmaid, but wilt give unto thy handmaid a man-child, then I will give him unto Jehovah all the days of his life, and there shall no razor come upon his head. (1 Samuel 1:9-11 ASV)

Focus on these words in 1 Samuel 1:9, "So Hannah **rose up** at Shiloh." She was in a situation year after year in which she had to go through this ridicule. We have to understand her position—day after day she had to endure this shame and mocking from the other wife of her husband. Because she was childless, her culture at that time saw her as essentially worthless. Within Hannah, a hurricane of emotions was brewing.

At times, we find it hard to even smile occasionally because of the storm raging inside of us. Battles, wars, struggles, temptations, conflicts, and terrible chaos often tear us apart as they rip asunder the very fabric of our souls. Our dreams have turned into nightmares. Instead of awakening refreshed, we greet the new day fatigued, depressed, and without the strength to rise up. Such an inner mayhem had been unleashed within Hannah. Yet, Hannah **rose up!**

What do you do when you are beaten down?
Where do you go when you're already in the basement?
When down is the only direction your emotions have been traveling,
Where is the staircase going up?

Hannah isn't the only example of a biblical character who reversed direction and started going up a *down* staircase.

Jacob was going down the road of fear and sibling rejection, and yes, running *down* the road to get as far away from home and family as possible after taking the blessing from his father that was meant for his brother. When going down, God gave him a dream with a staircase **GOING UP.** "And he lighted upon a certain place, and tarried there all night, because the sun was set; and he took one of the stones of the place, and put it under his head, and lay down in that place to sleep. And he dreamed; and, behold, a ladder set up on the earth, and the top of it reached to heaven; and, behold, the angels of God ascending and descending on it." Genesis 28:11-12). **Do you need to go up!** Arise from your nightmare and embrace God's dream. Go UP from your depression and despair to God's hope. Jacob was able to GO UP with God; so can you.

Similarly, after three days of fasting, Queen Esther rose up, put on her royal robes and went to take a stand in the king's hall. With the extension of the King's scepter to her, she would die. If she had stayed away, she and her people (the Jews) would have been massacred. She had to get up and **STAND UP** for what God wanted and others needed in order to be saved. **So you need to stand up for justice and what's right.** Like Hannah, Esther rose up from her grieving and was able to STAND UP to the enemy; so can you.

27

Levi, a sinner and a tax collector, —one of those Jewish IRS agents collecting taxes from his own people for the hated Romans —Levi **ROSE UP!**

He left his career, his wealth, and his position of power to follow an itinerant and wandering rabbi named Yeshua passing by, who said to Levi, "Follow me."

"And he [Levi] forsook all, and **rose up** and followed him [Jesus]" (Luke 5:28).

When Levi rose up he left behind his past, the scorn of others, the greed and pride that had driven him. His journey to redemption began. Years later, this same Levi whom we know as Matthew would pen a gospel bearing his name and impact billions of people throughout the centuries with his testimony about the Savior. Levi discovered that when he rose UP to follow Jesus, he left behind everything of his old ways, shameful sins, and wicked ways.

Like Levi, you need to RISE UP and leave behind all your past baggage and burdens in order to follow Jesus.

❧

If you're tired of your present situation, get up, go up, stand up, and rise up to seize the calling, the vision, the hope, and the future that God has reserved for you.

❧

It's Time for You to Rise UP!

Hannah rose UP. Esther rose UP. Levi rose UP. So if you're sick and tired of being sick and tired, get up. Have you ever seen a pig's sty? Do you know what they do there? Pigs wallow in the mud. They never get up, wipe themselves off, and take a shower. No, they enjoy wallowing in the mud just like some people seem to relish ...

... grieving instead of laughing, losing instead of winning, being a victim instead of a victor, and staying under their circumstances instead of RISING UP above them.

We must understand that if we're tired of our current situation, condition or circumstance, then we have to rise up like Hannah. We've got to **rise up and recognize** that there is a problem. The news flash is that if you don't rise up and do something about your situation, nobody is going to do it for you. It's time for each of us to acknowledge that we have a problem, and if we wallow in the mud for too long without rising up, we don't have a problem; we *are* the problem!

The biblical narrative about Hannah reads that she rose up after they had eaten in Shiloh. Please note that Shiloh in the original text means "a place of rest." Some of us have been resting in a place too long. Some of us have been resting in our situations too long; others have been resting in our circumstances too long, and some have been resting in our comfort zones too long. Too many of us have been resting in our mess and our foolishness for far too long. Some of us even rest in trivial stuff. It is time for all of us to do like Hannah did and **RISE UP**! out of our present situation.

Suzan Johnson Cook, the U.S. Ambassador-at-Large for International Religious Freedom from 2011 to 2015, distinguished African American bestselling author and American Baptist pastor, wrote a dynamic book about rising UP in our lives titled *Moving Up: Dr. Sujay's Ten Steps to Turning Your Life Around and Getting to the Top!* (Doubleday Religion; 2008). She writes that if we are stuck (like wallowing in the mud) we need to start moving up. Those ten steps are:

- Stand Up!
- Speak Up!
- Rise Up!
- Look Up!
- Book Up!
- Kiss Up!
- Listen Up!

- Hang Up!
- Make Up!
- Cheer Up!

Yes, we must stand up and speak up like Esther did. We have to look up as Jacob did. We have to rise up and listen up when Jesus says "follow me," as Levi (Matthew) did. And, in order to rise up like Hannah we must learn how to *hang up*.

Hang up on all those lies of the enemy like:

You'll never have a baby.
No mate for you.
Quit on that dream God gave you,
You'll never have joy in the morning only tears all day and
*   night long.*
Forget about cheering up; no one is there to be your fan
*   or your BFF.*
Those folks you hurt, they'll never forgive you and make up.
And, might as well not book up, you're not smart enough to
*   ever get that education, promotion, or new job.*

Hannah refused to believe the father of lie and the enemy of her soul. The child she was standing up and speaking up for, Samuel, would not only serve God but also become one of the greatest judges and prophets in history. But if Hannah had not risen up from her sorrow, grief, and tears, she would never have been able to stand up to Eli or speak up for God's dream in her life.

So, let me ask you, "What's keeping you from RISING UP?"

Nothing Can Keep You *Down*

I've often wondered why God's people stay *down ... depressed ... dejected ... deluded ... and dead to their hopes and dreams.* Because Jesus ROSE UP! from the grave conquering sin and death, why don't we rise UP like Hannah did? Consider carefully what the Apostle Paul wrote to us,

What shall we say then? Shall we continue in sin, that grace may abound? God forbid. We who died to sin, how shall we any longer live therein? Or are ye ignorant that all we who were baptized into Christ Jesus were baptized into his death? We were buried therefore with him through baptism unto death: that like as Christ was raised from the dead through the glory of the Father, so we also might walk in newness of life. (Romans 6:1-4 ASV)

Let's look once more at Hannah's rising up. Instead of staying stuck in her barrenness and grieving in her spirit, she rose up and went into God's presence, petitioning God for what she needed. She didn't demand. She simply asked; asking the One who was able to bring life out of death in her body.

She knew that God was God of the new not the old. Read again what Paul wrote, "Christ was raised from the dead through the glory of the Father, so we also might walk in newness of life." Christ was raised up so we might rise up and walk in God's new plan, purpose, dream, and calling on our lives. God wants to raise you up from the old plans into His new plans for you. How does that happen?

1. **Recognize** that you're stuck! One must realize that recognition also involves repentance. You may need to repent of sin and transgressions in your life and seek the forgiving love of God in Christ. He will forgive you. 1 John 1:9 declares, "If we confess our sin he is faithful and righteous to forgive us our sins, and to cleanse us from all unrighteousness." Now, in Hannah's case, she did not have past sin to repent, but she did have to turn completely away from her resentment, depression, grief, and dejection. Repent is to make a 180-degree turn away from the past, the old, the plan, the mindset, feeling or behavior that's not lining up with God's will and way for your life. Whatever it is that's keeping you *down*, recognize it, confess it, repent from it, and turn toward God.

2. **Rise Up!** Faith without works is dead. Saying you trust God with your new walk with Christ and then sitting around doing nothing is sin. "Therefore to him who knows what is good (right) and does not do it, to him it is sin" (James 4:17). Hannah rose up and made a vow. She did what she knew to do as part of her Jewish tradition. It was the right thing for her. So, what is God's Spirit asking you to do, where is God in Christ asking you to go, and what is the next step of obedience you must take to walk in newness of life? Yes, it's risky. But remember, God orders the steps of a righteous person. His Word is a lamp to your feet and a light to your path. Do what Levi did; rise UP and follow Christ where he is leading you. Jesus' sheep know his voice and obey his commands.

Hannah also stayed within the house of God, the Tabernacle, and she listened to her priest. Stay rooted and grounded in the Church, the body of Christ. Get wise counsel. Walk with the saints who are following Jesus.

When Paul was knocked off his horse on the road to Damascus by the Risen Lord and blinded, what did he do? He repented. He stopped persecuting Christians. He went to a place where believers were gathered and listened to a faithful saint giving him guidance and counsel on what next steps he needed to take to keep walking in the right direction. Follow his example, Paul wrote, as he followed Christ.

3. **Release the old; revert to God's new.** Hannah refused to hold on to her past with its resentment, rejection, and ridicule. She focused on the God of the new. God is speaking to you right now these powerful words of release giving you the courage to revert to his new thing:

Behold, I will do a new thing,
Now it shall spring forth;
Shall you not know it?
I will even make a road in the wilderness
And rivers in the desert.
(Isaiah 43:19 NKJV)

Be Strong, Be Courageous—Rise UP!

Finally, step back a moment and look at what Hannah did in her rising up. She was a woman in a culture where women were viewed more as property than equals to men. She was in a religious system that ignored her worth and preciousness to God. She could have accepted the role in which her culture caste her and chosen not to RISE UP or SPEAK UP.

Nevertheless, she had the *chutzpah* (a Jewish Yiddish word for *gall, audacity, nerve*) to see herself as a child of God, loved and cherished by the God of Abraham, Isaac, and Jacob, the God and Father of our Lord Jesus Christ. Something in her DNA that told her she was created in the image and likeness of God ROSE UP in her and gave her the strength and courage to RISE UP and SPEAK UP.

You, child of God, woman or man, young person or old person, know that you are a new creation in Christ Jesus. Like Hannah, Esther, Jacob, Levi, and Paul, you have the courage and strength to RISE UP! Hear the God of Hannah say to you:

Strength! Courage!
Don't be timid;
Don't get discouraged.
God, your God, is with you every step you take!
(Joshua 1:9 MSG)

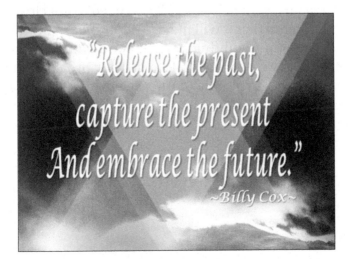

Chapter 3

Get to the Anointing

I press toward the mark for the prize of the high calling of God in Christ Jesus. (Philippians 3:14)

N ow you may be asking, "How in the world can I rise up out of this current situation?" I'm going to tell you according to Scripture. Eli the priest was sitting at the door or the entrance into the temple. I can only imagine Hannah saying, "I just need to get to the temple. I just need to get to the door. I just need to get to the place where there is an anointing that will make a different in my life."

Yes, I imagine Hannah saying, "I just need to get close enough to the anointing so that it will make a difference in my life. If I get close enough to the anointing it will make a difference in my life."

'This is how 'we become able to get our breakthrough. This is how we're going to be able to release whatever God has for us.

❧

We must go to where the anointing is.

❧

> *She was in bitterness of soul, and prayed unto the*
> *Lord, and wept sore.* (1 Samuel 1:10)

The word *sore* in the original text means "profoundly." The words "wept sore" together mean that through her intense weeping Hannah was able to *release something*. So if I'm going to cry that means there is something on the inside that has to come forth to the outside. If I'm going to weep, that means I'm going to keep pouring out the tears until it comes out because whatever hinders us from getting to the anointing does not belong there.

Before We Go, We Must Release

I wrote earlier in this book that *in order to release we must go to the right place*. So, the antecedent or precedent action to going is releasing. Before we start going, we must release. However, that release to go can only be toward one place—the right place of God's anointing. Let's look at the actions we must take in obedience in order to go:

1. Releasing the past
2. Moving toward the anointing

Releasing the past. Understand that the past does not determine your future or define you. Yes, Hannah shed tears over her past hurt, wounding, victimization, and pain. But, she didn't camp out there or allow a negative past to imprison her, nor did her hurtful past define her identity. She wasn't the "barren wife" or the "mocked woman." What others have said about you or done to you can never become who you are. What defines you isn't what others have spoken or done to you. Your identity rests in who God declares you are!

Releasing your past allows you not to focus on past successes to the degree that you become trapped in pride or self-centeredness. Release frees you to receive God's provisions and blessings in your present and in your future. One of those blessings is "no regrets." Motivational speaker Zig Ziglar asks us an important question, "Will you look back on life and say, 'I wish I had' or 'I'm glad I did'?"

When you let a painful past shape your present and determine your future, you rob your future of hope, potential, and anointed possibilities. What are some ways that you can release the past? Let me share with you just a few examples from the Scriptures.

First, *reject offense*. Jesus makes it clear that offenses will come. Look at how the Jewish leaders were offended by Jesus, but He rejected their offensive accusations, words, and actions. Instead of reacting with offense, Jesus responded with forgiveness. Carefully read His instructions:

> *Then He said to the disciples, "It is impossible that no offenses should come, but woe to him through whom they do come! It would be better for him if a millstone were hung around his neck, and he were thrown into the sea, than that he should offend one of these little ones. Take heed to yourselves. If your brother sins against you, rebuke him; and if he repents, forgive him. And if he sins against you seven times in a day, and seven times in a day returns to you, saying, 'I repent,' you shall forgive him."* (Luke 17:1-3 NKJV)

How do you know if you have forgiven those who have hurt, ridiculed, or offended you?

The symptoms of holding onto your past include becoming offended, hate, continuing to remember and reliving former pain, or simply staying stuck and not moving forward. Paul reminds us that we can do all things through Christ who strengthens us.

❧

**You can *get over it* [your past]
and *get to the anointing.***

❧

Another way you know you haven't forgiven and rejected past offenses is continually talking about them or feeling offended every time you see or think of the person(s) who hurt you. In others words, you are filled with self-pity and a "poor me" attitude. Holding on to past offenses will keep you from getting to the place of anointing. I encourage you to pray and cry out to God because releasing and healing is much needed in so many very sensitive and delicate situations. To do so reminds me of an old story.

> *A man fell over a cliff. As he fell, he reached out and grabbed hold of a bush growing out of the side of the rocky slope. As he hung there, he cried out, "God, catch me. Save me." A divine utterance came forth, "Let go."*
> *Filled with fear and doubt, the dangling man clutched the bush even harder trying to keep himself from falling. The divine voice asked, "Do you trust me?"*
> *"Yes," came the frightened man's reply.*
> *"Then, let go," the voice replied.*
> *As much as the man protested that he had faith, he never let go ... he never obeyed.*

Faith without obedience, i.e. works, is dead ... and so ultimately was that man. Finally losing his strength, he lost his grip and fell to his death never knowing if faith would have saved him.

We cling to our past selves, our self-made identities, never trusting God with our present or our future, and never realizing how much simply releasing the past can empower our future. God created us in his image. Christ in us makes us a new creation—the old is passing away and all things are becoming new. Rejecting the offenses of the past can release us into God's identity for us—an identity filled with limitless possibilities.

Next, *respond with forgiveness.* You read the text. Forgiveness cuts off the past and releases our anger, pain, hurt, and bruised spirit. There is restoration and renewing in forgiveness for us. The only person unforgiveness hurts is the one who refuses to forgive. Reject the bait of Satan, i.e. offense. Respond with forgiveness.

Start with forgiving God. Not that He has done anything wrong. Rather, stop blaming him for the way the past has gone, others have hurt you, or the way he created you. Release blame and respond with forgiveness. Stop blaming God, others, or yourself for the offenses, mistakes, and failures of the past. If God forgives you, why do you keep condemning yourself and why do you keep replaying the situation over and over in your mind?

Deposit these truths into your spirit:

> *There is therefore now no condemnation to those who are in Christ Jesus, who do not walk according to the flesh, but according to the Spirit.* (Romans 8:1-2 NKJV)

> *Beloved, if our heart does not condemn us, we have confidence toward God. And whatever we ask we receive from Him, because we keep His commandments and do those things that are pleasing in His sight. And this is His commandment: that we should believe on the name of His Son Jesus Christ and love one another, as He gave us commandment.* (1 John 3:21-23 NKJV)

Now, *by rejecting offense* and *responding with forgiveness,* you are ready to *move toward the anointing.* In the book *The Bait of Satan: Living Free From the Deadly Trap of Offense* (Charisma House: 2014), author John Brevere shares a powerful story of how releasing past offense and unforgiveness moved two people into the anointing, the Presence of God.

> *Just before I [John Brevere] spoke, a burly, middle-aged man stood up before the congregation and wept [like Hannah] as he relayed his tragic story: "All my life I have felt like there was a wall between me and God. I would attend meetings where others sensed God's presence, while I watched detached and numbed. Even while I prayed there was no*

release or presence. Several weeks ago I was handed "The Bait of Satan." I read it in its entirety. I realized I had taken Satan's bait years ago. I hated my mother. I hated my mother for abandoning me when I was six months old. I realized I had to go to her and forgive. I called and spoke with her for only the second time in thirty-six years.... I forgave her and she forgave herself; now we are reconciled." Then came the exciting part. "Now the wall that separated me from God's presence is gone!"[1]

Move Toward the Anointing

For Hannah, releasing the past and moving forward with her life meant getting in the place where the anointing was—the tabernacle of the Most High God. She went there to pray. At that time, the Presence of God, the anointing of His Presence, rested over the Ark of the Covenant in the Holy of Holies. There she could boldly approach God's presence in prayer.

As believers, we can go to a heavenly tabernacle with a risen High Priest—Christ the Lord. Read the truth according to Scripture:

> *Seeing then that we have a great High Priest who has passed through the heavens, Jesus the Son of God, let us hold fast our confession. For we do not have a High Priest who cannot sympathize with our weaknesses, but was in all points tempted as we are, yet without sin. Let us therefore come boldly to the throne of grace, that we may obtain mercy and find grace to help in time of need. (Hebrews 4:14-16)*

What keeps you from boldly approaching the throne of Christ's grace? Check the following issues that block your movement toward the anointed One and His grace?
- Shame
- Offense
- Fear

- Guilt
- Lack of Confidence
- Regret
- Sorrow
- Pride
- Unforgiveness
- Rejection

You have nothing to fear, nothing to hide, and nothing to lose by releasing the past and moving toward the anointing. The anointed one, Jesus Christ, invites you through his mercy and grace to approach him with any request, any petition, any confession, and any repentance. With tears and godly sorrow, like Hannah had, come boldly to Christ and experience the anointing of Christ's presence. He will freely forgive, freely forget, and freely release you from the past into an anointed future full of power, confidence, and boldness. What are you waiting for? Be like Hannah. *Get to the anointing, now!* Let the words of the familiar hymn be your prayer right now...

> *Just as I am–Thou wilt receive,*
> *Wilt welcome, pardon, cleanse, relieve;*
> *Because Thy promise I believe,*
> *-O Lamb of God, I come!*
>
> *Just as I am–Thy love unknown*
> *Has broken every barrier down;*
> *Now to be Thine, yea, Thine alone,*
> *-O Lamb of God, I come!*
>
> *Just as I am–of that free love*
> *The breadth, length, depth, and height to prove,*
> *Here for a season, then above,*
> *-O Lamb of God, I come!*
> (Charlotte Elliott, 1835)

"You can't reach for anything new if your hands are still full of yesterday's junk."

~Author: Louie Smith~

Chapter 4

Declare to Release

And she [Hannah] *was in bitterness of soul, and prayed to the Lord and wept in anguish. Then she made a vow and said, "O Lord of hosts, if You will indeed look on the affliction of Your maidservant and remember me, and not forget Your maidservant, but will give Your maidservant a male child, then I will give him to the Lord all the days of his life, and no razor shall come upon his head." (1 Samuel 1:10-11 NKJV)*

I am going to piggyback on what the old Saints use to say: "I do declare. I do declare that today is a day of miracles. I do declare that today is going to be a day of release. I do declare that today is going to be a day that we'll receive what God has in store for us."

When Hannah got to the tabernacle, she went to the place of God's anointing and released all the years of anger. I believe she also released all the years of bitterness. Furthermore, I think she released all the years of the foolishness that she had to go through *and* the aggravation *and* the wrath *and* the resentment *and* the adversity *and* the difficulties *and* the tribulations, *and beyond all that,* I also believe she released depression.

I believe that there are too many folks who are claiming their depression. We need to release that negative thought, feeling, or memory today, once and for all. If Hannah could release it, that means you can release it. (Those who are diagnosed with clinical depression, which is a serious mental illness, can release it through prayer and by prayerfully seeking therapy and/or medical treatment.)

You can release the anger,
> *you can release the bitterness,*
>> *you can release the foolishness,*
> *you can release the wrath, resentment, adversity, difficulty, tribulations, and*
>> *you can release the depression.*

As a preacher and counselor to many through my ministry, I have observed what so many Christian psychologists, counselors, and psychiatrists have observed:

ॐ

At the root of depression is bitterness.
The root of bitterness springs out of anger.
Ultimately all anger, bitterness, and depression
are directed toward blaming God and others
for life's tribulations.

ॐ

Releasing Depression, Bitterness, Blame and Anger

I see it often in worship services at the altar. People come and ask for prayer so that they might be emotionally healed. "I suffer from depression, grief, and sadness," they declare. What they declare is what they continue to sow into the terrain or soil of their souls. That seed they are declaring proceeds to bear the fruit of their words. In Proverbs 18:21, we read that our tongues are either sowing life or death. In Corinthians, Paul writes that whatever we sow we will reap. Seed we have sown into our hearts as the result of our responses to life's difficulties will bear the fruit we have spoken.

Let me help you understand this with a parable from Jesus and an understanding of how sowing and reaping works in our hearts, our inner man—the human spirit. Carefully read aloud the Parable of the Sower that Jesus tells in Mark 4:3-20 MSG).

> *"Listen. What do you make of this? A farmer planted seed. As he scattered the seed, some of it fell on the road and birds ate it. Some fell in the gravel; it sprouted quickly but didn't put down roots, so when the sun came up it withered just as quickly. Some fell in the weeds; as it came up, it was strangled among the weeds and nothing came of it. Some fell on good earth and came up with a flourish, producing a harvest exceeding his wildest dreams.*
>
> *"Are you listening to this? Really listening?"*
>
> *When they were off by themselves, those who were close to him, along with the Twelve, asked about the stories. He told them, "You've been given insight into God's kingdom — you know how it works. But to those who can't see it yet, everything comes in stories, creating readiness, nudging them toward receptive insight. These are people —*
>
> > *Whose eyes are open but don't see a thing,*
> > *Whose ears are open but don't understand a word,*
> > *Who avoid making an about-face and getting forgiven."*
>
> *He continued, "Do you see how this story works? All my stories work this way.*
>
> *"The farmer plants the Word. Some people are like the seed that falls on the hardened soil of the*

road. No sooner do they hear the Word than Satan snatches away what has been planted in them.

"And some are like the seed that lands in the gravel. When they first hear the Word, they respond with great enthusiasm. But there is such shallow soil of character that when the emotions wear off and some difficulty arrives, there is nothing to show for it.

"The seed cast in the weeds represents the ones who hear the kingdom news but are overwhelmed with worries about all the things they have to do and all the things they want to get. The stress strangles what they heard, and nothing comes of it.

"But the seed planted in the good earth represents those who hear the Word, embrace it, and produce a harvest beyond their wildest dreams."

I quoted the parable for you from The Message Bible just so you might hear it in a fresh way. Words are like seed. Our hearts are the soil within us upon which seed fall. Our hearts can become hardened soil. How does that happen?

When we respond to life's difficulties with negative declarations (spoken or thought words), we sow seeds of "death" into our hearts. They bear fruit of the flesh not of the spirit. That fruit manifests as anger, bitterness, grief, and depression. What we sow, we reap. As Paul wrote,

"Do not be deceived, God is not mocked; for whatever a man sows, that he will also reap. For he who sows to his flesh will of the flesh reap corruption, but he who sows to the Spirit will of the Spirit reap ever-lasting life. And let us not grow weary while doing good, for in due season we shall reap if we do not lose heart. Therefore, as we have opportunity, let

us do good to all, especially to those who are of the household of faith." (Galatians 6:7-10 NKJV)

In Matthew 15, Jesus reminds us that it is out of our hearts that the mouth speaks. If we have declared and thus sown the word of God into our hearts, then the fruit of that word, the fruit of the Spirit will come out. Paul writes in Galatians 5:22-23 that the fruit of the Spirit is "love, joy, peace, longsuffering, kindness, goodness, faithfulness, gentleness, self-control."

Any word we speak into our spirit man other than God's word birthed from His Spirit bears bad fruit and issues out of our mouths from our hearts as negative declarations. Those declarations become seed sown back into our hearts (and into the hearts of others) which, in turn, continue to take root in the terrain of our souls producing thorns, weeds, and rocky or hardened soil making us more resistant to God's words or seed of the Spirit. We need to break this destructive cycle which robs both our present and future of God's hope, joy, and blessings. How do we root out depression, anger, and bitterness? Let me show you!

Declare to Release

Declaring is sowing words of life into the terrain of our souls so that the harvest from God of the Spirit's fruit can come into our lives and be sown into the lives of others around us. Hannah got to the anointing and declared before the Presence of God, *"O Lord of hosts, if You will indeed look on the affliction of Your maidservant and remember me, and not forget Your maidservant, but will give Your maidservant a male child, then I will give him to the Lord all the days of his life, and no razor shall come upon his head"* (1 Samuel 1:11 NKJV). She was sowing all she had to the Lord. Isn't that how God gives to us—He gave is only begotten son. Hannah was giving her only begotten son to God.

When we *declare to release,* we often go about our declaration the wrong way. We speak, declare, and want to release all the pain, hurt, depression, anger, blame, and bitterness to the Lord. It's important to make note of what Hannah did not declare. She did not rehearse all the terrible things said and done to her by her family, faith, and friends. If she had, she would have released a huge amount of negative seed into the soil of her soul. Yes, there was a root of bitterness in her tears of anguish. Ephesians 4:31-32 instructs, "Let all bitterness, wrath, anger, clamor, and evil speaking be put away from you, with all malice. And be kind to one another, tenderhearted, forgiving one another, even as God in Christ forgave you."

❧

Declaring what's wrong with your past never puts you right with God.

❧

Consider how often your prayers have been an unending litany to God about all that's going wrong in your life. You expect God to rapture you out of the world because you are petitioning Him with weeping. But Jesus says, "These things I have spoken to you, that in Me you may have peace. In the world you will have tribulation; but be of good cheer, I have overcome the world" (John 16:33). You are in the world, not of the world. Therefore, stop responding to life's difficulties with an attitude of depression, anger, and bitterness. Instead, declare to release. Be of good cheer. Have an attitude of gratitude. God responds to positive declarations that release His promises into your life. How do you declare to release?

Declarations That Release Your Past & Sow Hope into Your Future

Remember that Hannah lived in a Jewish culture that worshipped *Elohim,* who spoke destiny, hope, and purpose into Adam and Eve by saying, "Be fruitful and multiply." We have already learned that the fruit we bear springs forth from the seed we sow. Sow depression, reap it. Sow hope, reap it. Sow curses, reap curses. Sow promises, reap the fruit of God's promises. In Christ, the promises of God are *yes* and *amen.* Hannah knew she was created to be fruitful. So her prayer declared her hope for a child rooted in God's promise to her and all women in bearing children. She declared what God wanted for her, not simply what she wanted. She aligned her expectations of God with the design God had for her. She sowed out of the fruit of the Spirit not out of the desires of the flesh. She declared to release what God wanted for the future.

✌

**Declare what God wants to release into your
body, soul, and future
to prosper you and give you hope.**

✌

What do we declare to release? We declare God's established words, plans, and promises for us. God reminds us in Jeremiah 29:11, "For I know the plans I have for you," declares the Lord, "plans to prosper you and not to harm you, plans to give you a hope and a future." Learn from God. What does He declare to release? He declares His divine will, plans, and purposes for you to bring you into a future filled with prosperity and hope.

Declare your agreement with God's plans for your future.
  Declare the release of His promises for yourself, your family and friends.
    Declare the forty, sixty, and hundredfold release for your finances.

Declare To Release!
At the beginning of this book, I started telling the story of a prisoner locked away. Here's a similar tale for you to ponder in this moment.
A revolutionary French citizen was captured in the early days of the French Revolution by the King's soldiers and thrown into the famous Bastille as a political prisoner. He was isolated and had no

contact with other prisoners or even his guards who shoved his food through an opening in the door but never spoke a word to him. As the days, weeks, and months past, he lost all hope and continually wept over the mistakes he had made that led to his capture.

One day, the food stopped coming and a note was passed through the opening in the door. It simply read, "You are free." He was so depressed, fearful, angry, and bitter, he could only imagine that the note was a cruel trick. The prisoner "just knew" that his captors wanted him to try to escape so that would have an excuse to shoot him on the spot.

Finally, one day the door opened. A smiling soldier said, "We had no idea you were still back here in this hole. You are free to go. You've been free to leave for months. The door has been unlocked. France has been liberated!"

Do you see the irony in this tale? The prisoner was only imprisoned by his mind, emotions, fears, and past. The door to his freedom and future was unlocked. He refused to believe the declaration of his release. Are you like this prisoner? Christ has unlocked the door that made you a prisoner to your past; you are free!

The truth is that every negative sin, failure, weakness, and mistake you made in the past does not hold you in bondage right now. Are you not a child of God? Are you not already saved, healed, and delivered by the Lord of Lord and King of Kings? You now walk in freedom and release from your past through the shed blood of Jesus Christ, who died for you on the cross. Never declare to release you from the past. That's been done in Christ. Give thanks. Rejoice. When you pray, pray with joy and thanksgiving. Philippians 4:4-7 declares:

> *Rejoice in the Lord always. I will say it again: Rejoice!*
> *Let your gentleness be evident to all. The Lord is near.*
> *Do not be anxious about anything,*
> *but in everything, by prayer and petition, with thanksgiving,*
> *present your requests to God.*

And the peace of God, which transcends all understanding,
will guard your hearts and your minds in Christ Jesus.
(NIV)

When you "declare to release," declare your requests with joy and thanksgiving for the past mercies and grace of God. What gets released? The peace of God. Hannah declared to release and what happened? Eli spoke the peace of God's promise, hope, and future over her.

Yes, God would have me to share with you the miracle that Hannah received when she released.

Wherefore it came to pass, when the time was come about after Hannah had conceived, that she bare a son, and called his name Samuel, saying, Because I have asked him of the Lord. (1 Samuel 1:20 KJV)

Make These Declarations to Release for Your Breakthrough

Now is the time for you to claim the release Christ bought for you on the cross from your tears of anguish, your depression, anger, and bitterness. Yes, this is the moment you take to heart the words of Hebrews 12:14-15 (NKJV):

Pursue peace with all people, and holiness,
without which no one will see the Lord:
looking carefully lest anyone fall short of the grace of God;
lest any root of bitterness springing up cause trouble,
and by this many become defiled.
Pull up the root of bitterness. Right now, and continually declare:

❧

My breakthrough is about to come to pass;
my deliverance is about to come pass.

❧

50

Scripture says that she was with child as soon as her breakthrough came to pass. Hannah bore a son and his name was Samuel. Our God is a miracle worker; our God is one who can make a way out of no way. He needs your confession, repentance, surrender, cooperation, and declarations to open a door for Him to sow all of His plans to prosper you and give you hope into the surrendered soil of your soul.

Declare to release!

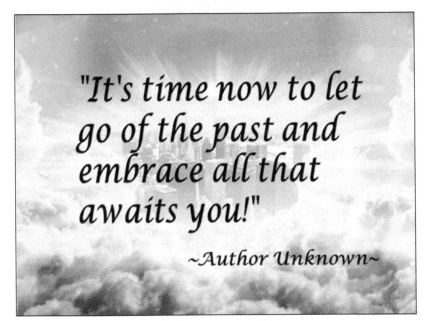

"It's time now to let go of the past and embrace all that awaits you!"

~Author Unknown~

Chapter 5

From Release to Breakthrough

Now it came about, as she continued praying before the Lord, that Eli was watching her mouth.

As for Hannah, she was speaking in her heart, only her lips were moving, but her voice was not heard. So Eli thought she was drunk.

Then Eli said to her, "How long will you make yourself drunk? Put away your wine from you."

But Hannah replied, "No, my lord, I am a woman oppressed in spirit; I have drunk neither wine nor strong drink, but I have poured out my soul before the Lord. Do not consider your maidservant as a worthless woman, for I have spoken until now out of my great concern and provocation."

Then Eli answered and said, "Go in peace; and may the God of Israel grant your petition that you have asked of Him."

She said, "Let your maidservant find favor in your sight." So the woman went her way and ate, and her face was no longer sad. (1 Samuel 1:12-18)

When you release all the past and what holds you back, you will be able to receive the miracle that God has in store for your life. When you release anger, you will be able to receive your anointing. When you release bitterness, you will be able to receive your blessing. When you release demonic ways, you will be able to receive your deliverance. When you release gossiping, you will be able to receive God's way that He wants you to do things. When you release jealousy, you will be able to receive joy. When you release sexual sins, you will be able to receive the promises from God. When you release your vulgar mindset, you will be able to receive the victory in Jesus in every area of your life.

We must reach the point where we are able to move from the battle to the breakthrough. We'll be able to release the weights and be able to have wings where we can fly to the different heights to which God has called us to fly. When we release that aggravated situation, God will elevate us to the next level.

In his book, *God the Entrepreneur,* Dr. Buddy Crum of Life Center Ministries in Atlanta describes Kingdom business as a movement from Perspective to Process to People which produces Product. I want to repurpose and apply these concepts for understanding how we move from release to breakthrough.

Focus, Fight, Finish!

Hannah moved beyond a fixation on her grief, her lack, and her family difficulties to a focus on God. She had to get to the anointing. Her eyes had to be fixed on the Problem-Solver not the problem. She realized that she could no longer wallow in the weight of her sorrow. She needed a breakthrough. When she changed her focus to God's presence at the Tabernacle that has as its central focus the Holy of Holies, then Hannah's perspective shifted from problem to Presence, from turmoil and strife, to the peace that passes all understanding.

❧

When you focus on God's Presence, Your Perspective is on things above not below.

❧

Release comes from above not below. You are the head not the tail. God's promise to you is that your position is one of release not bondage, of being lifted up not being put down: "The Lord will make you the head and not the tail, and you only will be above, and you will not be underneath, if you listen to the commandments of the Lord your God, which I charge you today, to observe them carefully, and do not turn aside from any of the words which I command you today, to the right or to the left, to go after other gods to serve them." (Deuteronomy 28:13-14)

Your focus changes your *perspective* from looking down to looking up, from what's below your position in Christ—seated in the heavenlies on the right hand of God—to what's above. Listen to the words of Paul:

> "If then you were raised with Christ, seek those things which are **above**, where Christ is, sitting at the right hand of God. Set your mind on things **above**, not on things on the earth. For you died, and your life is hidden with Christ in God. When Christ who is our life appears, then you also will appear with Him in glory." (Colossians 3:1-4)

Think of your perspective looking down from the Empire State Building at the bustle, traffic jams, and congestion of Manhattan. You have ridden the high-speed elevator up. Released from the jam of people and problems below, you have risen above it all. Your perspective from 320 meters up is quite different from street level. You are not under the smog but above it. You can see far into the distance with a 360-degree view. 'It appears as though you are above the things of earth.

It's impossible to move from release to breakthrough until you rise above the people, problems, and pressures that weigh you down. When first going to the Empire State Building, you must first fight through the traffic, fight for a place to park, fight through the throngs of people on the sidewalks, fight through sidewalk detours around construction, fight through the line of people waiting to get tickets to go up, fight your way into the jammed elevator, and fight your way out of the closed, window-less box that traps you too close to other people, until the doors finally open and you step into a place above it all, looking out in every direction. Ah, the view is magnificent and the things below have been left behind. Release, you are ready for a break-through. How then does your spiritual perspective change? You must sit at the right hand of God with Christ and lean on the everlasting arms.

What a fellowship, what a joy divine,
Leaning on the everlasting arms;
What a blessedness, what a peace is mine,
Leaning on the everlasting arms.

Refrain:
Leaning, leaning,
Safe and secure from all alarms;
Leaning, leaning,
Leaning on the everlasting arms.

Oh, how sweet to walk in this pilgrim way,
Leaning on the everlasting arms;
Oh, how bright the path grows from day to day,
Leaning on the everlasting arms.

What have I to dread, what have I to fear,
Leaning on the everlasting arms?
I have blessed peace with my Lord so near,
Leaning on the everlasting arms.
(Elisha A. Hoffman)

Fellowshipping with God the Father is your focus. Reread the passage from Colossians out loud, slowly, and change the person from second person to first person:

- *I have been raised with Christ.* You are looking up, going up, and focusing up.
- *I am seeking those things which are **above.*** I am not under my circumstances; I am over them. I can imagine Hannah once saying, "Under the circumstances that I am barren, rejected, mocked, and ridiculed, I am bound by depression, sorrow, and grief." But once she focused on getting to the anointing, into God's Presence, her perspective changed, and she was released from the past and positioned to receive her breakthrough.
- *I have been elevated to sit where Christ is seated—at the right hand of God.* I see all of life from above not below. I have God's perspective, not my own, the world's, or other people's viewpoints. I am lifted up not put down. Released from all earthly cares, I can see the solutions and find the answers that God has instead of being imprisoned by what seemed to be hopeless problems, difficulties, and dead-end directions.
- *My mind is set on things above, not on things on the earth.* You go where you focus. The focus is not on the battle. It's on God the Mighty Man of War who fights the battle on your behalf. The Lord of Hosts stands before you as He stood before Hannah and Joshua before her. Remember when the children of Israel under Joshua's leadership, approached what seemed the impenetrable fortress of Jericho? As he focused on the coming battle, the captain of the Host of the Lord stood before him. He fixed his eyes on the theophany, or embodiment, of Jesus Christ. Read afresh what happened:

*Now it came about when Joshua was by Jericho, that **he lifted up his eyes and looked,** and behold, a man was standing opposite him with his sword drawn in his hand, and Joshua went to him and said*

*to him, "Are you for us or for our adversaries?" He
said, "No; rather I indeed come now as captain of
the host of the Lord." And Joshua fell on his face to
the earth, and bowed down, and said to him, "What
has my lord to say to his servant?" The captain of
the Lord's host said to Joshua, "Remove your san-
dals from your feet, for the place where you are
standing is holy." And Joshua did so.* (Joshua 5:13-
14, emphasis mine.)

At that moment, Joshua's perspective changed. The reve-
lation was that the battle belonged to the Lord (1 Samuel
17:47; 1 Chronicles 20:15). When Eli spoke peace to
Hannah in the Tabernacle, her perspective changed from
the battle—from fighting and turmoil—to peace. The God
of Peace was fighting her battles for her.

- *I have died to self; my life is hidden with Christ in God.* Are
  you willing to die to yourself? To see your former self
  perish to start anew? To stop fighting your own battles
  and surrender the good fight to the Lord of Hosts? Paul
  wrote, "I have fought the good fight, finished the race, and
  kept the faith" (See 2 Timothy 2:4.) Focus—keep your
  eyes fixed on Christ. Surround yourself, yes hide yourself
  in the Lord of Lords, Captain of the angelic host of heaven.
  The battle belongs to Him, but only after you are released
  from the fray and set above it in heavenly places.
- *Christ is my life. I will appear with Him in glory.* The outcome of the fight is already determined. In Christ, you
  are destined to win—to move from release to glorious
  breakthrough.
  You **focus** on Christ, **fight** through the mundane to the
  miraculous—from below to above—and then **finish** strong.

Right Perspective, Right Process, and Right People Help You Finish Strong

Your breakthrough is on the other side of your obedience, surrender, and dying to self. You are marching through the enemy's

territory, breaking through every obstacles and hindrance, and rising above the battle. You will break through and finish strong.

In his book *Finishing Strong: Going the Distance for Your Family (Multnomah; 2000),* author Steve Farrar tells the story of three Christian "stars" who came on the scene in 1945, demonstrating the principles of finishing strong. Billy Graham was filling auditoriums and stadiums across American with as many as 30,000 people at a time. With his fiery, evangelistic preaching, Graham was leading thousands to repentance and faith in Jesus Christ. Surely you have heard of him and how strongly he has finished for Christ while staying above the crowds of fallen preachers and TV evangelists.

But have you heard of the other two stars who were Graham's contemporaries? Chuck Templeton was a colleague of Graham's, starting out with him in the international Youth for Christ organization. In fact, magazines at the time talked about Templeton's impact for Christ, never mentioning Graham. One seminary president called Templeton, not Graham, the most gifted preacher of his time. Yet, only five years later in 1950, Templeton left ministry to become a radio and television commentator and stated that he no longer believed in the claims of Jesus Christ.

Bron Clifford was also a star in 1945. He too preached to thousands of people leading many to Christ. One crusade he held in Miami was so packed with people trying to get into it that they lined up ten and twelve deep trying to get in. The president at Baylor University dismissed classes so that students could attend Clifford's lectures on "Christ and the Philosopher's Stone." Clifford, Templeton, and Graham all started out strong but how did they finish?

> *Graham, Templeton, and Clifford. In 1945, all three came shooting out of the starting blocks like rockets. You've heard of Billy Graham. So how come you've never heard of Chuck Templeton or Bron Clifford? Especially when they came out of the chutes so strong in '45. Just five years later, Templeton left the ministry to pursue a career as a radio and television*

commentator and newspaper columnist. Templeton had decided he was no longer a believer in Christ in the orthodox sense of the term. By 1950, this future Babe Ruth wasn't even in the game and no longer believed in the validity of the claims of Jesus Christ. What about Clifford? By 1954, Clifford had lost his family, his ministry, his health, and then... his life. Alcohol and financial irresponsibility had done him in. He wound up leaving his wife and their two Down's syndrome children. At just thirty-five years of age, this once great preacher died from cirrhosis of the liver in a run-down motel on the edge of Amarillo. His last job was selling used cars in the panhandle of Texas. He died, as John Haggai put it, "unwept, unhonored, and unsung." Some pastors in Amarillo took up a collection among themselves in order to purchase a casket so that his body could be shipped back East for decent burial in a cemetery for the poor. In 1945, three young men with extraordinary gifts were preaching the gospel to multiplied thousands across this nation. Within ten years, only one of them was still on track for Christ. In the Christian life, it's not how you start that matters. It's how you finish.[2]

In order to finish strong—to move from release to breakthrough—we need the right perspective, process, and people. The perspective is with Christ, seated with Him in heavenly places. The process is setting our mind on things above not below. Hannah had to do it. Joshua did it. When facing the crucifixion, Jesus did it, praying, "Thy will not mine be done." You can do it. Move beyond the battle.

What about the people around you? When your perspective is above not below, some of the people around you will have to change or you cannot take them with you. Pleasing people cannot be your focus.

We are pleasing God, not man. Hannah was not focused on pleasing her husband, or the other woman, or those in the village around her. She kept her faith, her focus, in God not man. Without faith, it's impossible to please God. By faith, Hannah kept moving from release to breakthrough. Her breakthrough came when she got to the place of anointing and into the Presence of God.

Are there people around you who are holding you back, hindering you from God's breakthrough for you?

ઌ

Declare to release so that you can move into your breakthrough.

ઌ

Declare Psalm 1 over your life. Until you are released from the negative, critical, mockers, and skeptical people around you, God's breakthrough for you will never arrive. The right perspective, process, and people will produce the prosperity and peace you need to live a victorious life. Read it to move from release to breakthrough. Then declare this daily, act upon this declaration daily, and receive your breakthrough.

> *How blessed I am when I do not walk in the counsel of the wicked,*
> *Nor stand in the path of sinners,*
> *Nor sit in the seat of scoffers!*
>
> *But my delight is in the law of the Lord,*
> *And in His law I meditate day and night.*
>
> *I will be like a tree firmly planted by streams of water,*
> *Which yields its fruit in its season*
> *And its leaf does not wither;*
> *And in whatever I do, I prosper.*
> *(Psalm 1, adapted)*

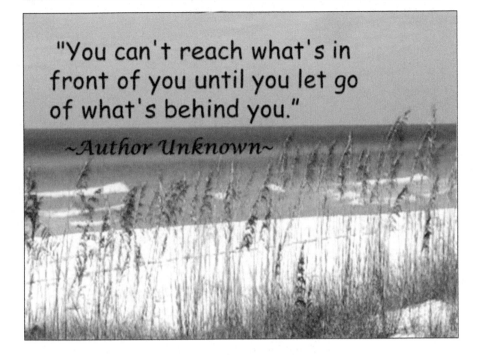

Chapter 6

Get to the Root

Her rival, however, would provoke her bitterly to irritate her, because the Lord had closed her womb. It happened year after year, as often as she went up to the house of the Lord, she would provoke her; so she wept and would not eat. Then Elkanah her husband said to her, "Hannah, why do you weep and why do you not eat and why is your heart sad? Am I not better to you than ten sons?" (1 Samuel 1:6-8)

I f we are to be released to our breakthrough, we must take an important action in the process of moving forward with God. *It's essential for us to get to the root!* When Hannah was provoked by her rival, Elkanah's other wife who had borne children "would provoke her bitterly to irritate her." Before Hannah could get to the anointing and come into God's Presence, she was provoked to what? We can read between the lines of this text and see various feelings within Hannah. I had a preacher friend who would say, "The more you stir it, the more it stinks."

That was the case with Hannah. Her rival would stir up all the feelings of rejection, lack, hurt, bitterness, anger, sorrow, and grief within Hannah. What a distraction from Hannah's focus on God's purpose and provision for her.

As long as the root of anger and bitterness was in Hannah, she could never go forward with God's plans, purpose, and prosperity for her life. In this chapter, let's get to the root of your anger and bitterness, as Hannah had to do, and when we get there, extract it like a bad, rotten, and decayed tooth.

Don't you hate tooth pain? When a cavity begins to grow, an infection penetrates the tooth and begins to affect the root of your tooth. The sugar silently eating away at your tooth's enamel now goes deep within your tooth to infect It with a cavity and cause distracting pain. So, you look for relief. At first you take over-the-counter pain killers. They help for a while. But the infection hasn't been eradicated. After a while, the pain doesn't diminish; it increases ... ouch!

Finally, you try some leftover antibiotics and pain killers you have in the medicine cabinet. Why? You hate going to the dentist. The pain of treatment and healing must be avoided if possible, or so you reason. For a while, the symptoms subside. You feel better. You ignore the root of the problem, which is causing the pain. The decay continues; the cavity grows. The pain comes back. Yuk!

Finally, your spouse, family member, or work colleague notices you wincing in pain when you eat a meal and says, "Why don't you do something about that tooth pain? Get to the root of the pain or it will only get worse. Go to the dentist!"

Reluctantly, "like pulling teeth" as they say, you pick up the phone, call the dentist's office and make an appointment. When you go into the office and settle into the chair, you are anxious. You fear both what the dentist will find and what it will cost. More than both of those fears, you are afraid that the dentist will find something worse than just a cavity to be filled. Sure enough, your worst fears are realized. The tooth's root is infected beyond healing. You need a root canal. You have to extract that root and clean out the infection in order to save the tooth.

With your spiritual life and relationship with God, the infection of angry bitterness has grown beyond your ability to fix it. You must get to the root. An extraction of the root of bitterness must happen, *now!*

Dr. Izola Jones, an awesome woman of God, is also a Christian counselor based in Maryland. The first thing she says during a first session is, "I need you to think back as far back as you can remember. Think back to when you were growing up with mom and dad." The reason that she does this is because you've got to understand that all of us are a byproduct of our past. Everything that we have been through in our lives makes us who we are today. She takes you all the way back because if you never go back, you'll never be able to deal with the issues from where they started. You have to go to the root. In order to release to receive your breakthrough, you must get to the root. You must allow Christ to extract that ugliness and restore you to spiritual health, wholeness, holiness, and wellness.

❧

**To *release to receive* your breakthrough,
you must get to the root,
allow Christ to extract that ugliness and
restore you to spiritual health, wholeness, holiness,
and wellness.**

❧

Extracting the Root of Bitterness

The Scriptures are filled with references about the need to extract poisonous, bitter, and wicked roots from within us and around us in order to obey God's commands and walk in the way of righteousness. Here are some of those instructions to get to the root and extract or expunge it.

- ***Remove roots bearing poisonous fruit and wormwood*** "so that there will not be among you a man or woman, or family or tribe, whose heart turns away today from the Lord our God, to go and serve the gods of those nations; that there will not be among you a root bearing poisonous fruit and wormwood. "It shall be when he hears the words of this curse, that he will boast, saying, 'I have peace though I walk in the stubbornness of my heart in order to destroy the watered land with the dry.' "The Lord shall never be willing to forgive him, but rather the anger of the Lord and His jealousy will burn against that man, and every curse which is written in this book will rest on him, and the Lord will blot out his name from under heaven. "Then the Lord will single him out for adversity from all the tribes of Israel, according to all the curses of the covenant which are written in this book of the law." (Deuteronomy 29:18-21)

Is there someone like Hannah had in her life who poisons your thoughts and feelings, provoking you to grief, anger, and bitterness? Refuse to listen to them. Don't let such a person distract you from getting to the anointing and coming into God's presence in worship and prayer.

- ***Never let foolishness take root in you.*** "I have seen the foolish taking root, and I cursed his abode immediately" (Job 5:3). Listening to fools who disregard and disobey the ways and commands of God grows a root of foolishness in you. You begin to doubt God. A fool says in his heart, "God doesn't exist or isn't there for me."
Curse foolish thoughts. Ban them from your eyes, ears, lips, mind, and heart. Stay pure and focused on divine wisdom from above not foolish banter from below.

- ***Reject the root of wickedness and greed.*** "A man will not be established by wickedness, But the root of the righteous will not be moved ... The wicked man desires the booty of evil men, But the root of the righteous yields fruit" (Proverbs 12:3,12). Doing things the world's way leads to wickedness and destruction. Desiring what others have violates the tenth commandment which mandates that we do not covet. Refuse to allow a root of wickedness or greed grow in the soil of your soul.

- ***Purge from your life relationships that profane God.*** "'For behold, the day is coming, burning like a furnace; and all the arrogant and every evildoer will be chaff; and the day that is coming will set them ablaze,' says the Lord of hosts, 'so that it will leave them neither root nor branch. But for you who fear My name, the sun of righteousness will rise with healing in its wings; and you will go forth and skip about like calves from the stall. You will tread down the wicked, for they will be ashes under the soles of your feet on the day which I am preparing,' says the Lord of hosts" (Malachi 4:1-3). The day of your breakthrough is coming, but only if you cut loose those people who try to play God in your life telling you what to think, feel, and do. They should be encouraging you to follow Christ, not them.

As you learned in the last chapter, the righteous person in Psalm 1 stays away from the wicked, sinners, and scoffers. In doing so, the righteous become a tree of righteousness bearing good fruit. Who tempts you to be rooted with them by saying they are your friend, your family, your employer, and your source? Jesus reminds us that our family is comprised of those who do God's will: "For whoever does the will of My Father in heaven is My brother and sister and mother" (Matthew 12:50 NKJV).

- *Let no root of bitterness spring up that causes trouble.* "Pursue peace with all men, and the sanctification without which no one will see the Lord. See to it that no one comes short of the grace of God; that no root of bitterness springing up causes trouble, and by it many be defiled; that there be no immoral or godless person like Esau, who sold his own birthright for a single meal. For you know that even afterwards, when he desired to inherit the blessing, he was rejected, for he found no place for repentance, though he sought for it with tears" (Hebrews 12:14-18).

You may have a bad habit, an addictive behavior, an abusive relationship, a demeaning job, a personality-driven church, or a problem-driven mindset that causes you continuous trouble. That root of bitterness keeps you from receiving God's grace in your life. Instead of prosperity, you experience memories filled with lack, rejection, hurt, and pain. You need release to receive God's grace. Let go of the old memories and allow God's love, mercy, and grace for you to replace those roots of bitterness with His cleansing and purifying Presence.

I could list more passages, but you get the point. The Scriptures reveal, "The axe is already laid at the root of the trees; therefore every tree that does not bear good fruit is cut down and thrown in the fire" (Matthew 3:10). You must get to the root of your angry bitterness in order to identify the rotten root that must be pulled out and replaced by the root of righteousness. Getting to the root is not just about rooting out what's bad; it's also about getting to the root of righteousness.

Get to the Root of Righteousness

Many people reject and repent of a root of bitterness, but they do not replace the old, demonic cause of trouble. You cannot pull out the bad roots without sowing seeds of righteousness into your own house, your soul. Jesus teaches about this truth:

> *Now when the unclean spirit goes out of a man, it passes through waterless places seeking rest, and does not find it. Then it says, 'I will return to my house from which I came'; and when it comes, it finds it unoccupied, swept, and put in order. Then it goes and takes along with it seven other spirits more wicked than itself, and they go in and live there; and the last state of that man becomes worse than the first. That is the way it will also be with this evil generation.* (Matthew 12:43-45)

I have prayed with and for people like Hannah who come weeping to the house of God. They come to the altar wanting to be released; they cry out for deliverance from the past. Such people are desperate to be set free from past roots. However, all they want is relief, not repentance. Their godly sorrow doesn't produce change so that the righteous seed of God's truth can take root in their cleansed souls.

Hannah wanted more than relief from her torturous home life. She wanted a new thing, a child, a new birth, if you will. That baby boy that God gave Hannah is symbolic of what God wants for you. He wants to birth in you a root of righteousness that will bear good fruit in your life.

∾

True, godly sorrow that bring real repentance
births in us a root of righteousness
from which spring forth the fruit of God's Spirit.

∾

Real REPENTANCE – The Key to Your Release to Receive His Righteousness

Jesus opens His ministry in the Gospels with the announcement, "Repent for the Kingdom of heaven is at hand" (Matthew 3:2). After Pentecost and the powerful baptism of the Holy Spirit, Peter proclaims, "Repent, and each of you be baptized in the name of Jesus Christ for the forgiveness of your sins; and you will receive the gift of the Holy Spirit" (Acts 2:38).

Real repentance births in us a root of righteousness that is lasting and that changes us into the image of Christ. We become new creations. Let me help you understand the **Seven Marks of Real Repentance** that bring about more than relief from the past, but make you a new creation in Christ Jesus. The scripture text that unpacks the meaning of real repentance that leads to releasing your future in Christ is this:

> *Godly sorrow brings repentance that leads to salvation and leaves no regret, but worldly sorrow brings death. See what this godly sorrow has produced in you: what earnestness, what eagerness to clear yourselves, what indignation, what alarm,*

what longing, what concern, what readiness to see justice done. At every point you have proved your-selves to be innocent in this matter. (2 Corinthians 7:10-12 NKJV)

So, the marks of real repentance like the godly sorrow of Hannah are: (Make each point a declaration to release and receive from God.)

#1 – Earnestness
- *I am eager to clear myself with God.* Don't come reluctantly to repent. Refuse to be dragged to the altar.
- *I come running to repentance (to the altar).* Stop procrastinating. Never say, "Tomorrow is my day of salvation." Today is the day of salvation, deliverance, and healing for you.
- *I am weeping earnest tears of sorrow.* We say to children, "Stop crying those crocodile tears." Fake winning doesn't fool anyone least of all God. Get real and raw. Hannah was sobbing from the depths of her soul. Make this your song of repentance:

Just as I am, without one plea,
But that Thy blood was shed for me,
And that Thou bidst me come to Thee,
O Lamb of God, I come, I come.

Just as I am, and waiting not
To rid my soul of one dark blot,
To Thee whose blood can cleanse each spot,
O Lamb of God, I come, I come.

Just as I am, though tossed about
With many a conflict, many a doubt,
Fightings and fears within, without,
O Lamb of God, I come, I come.

Just as I am, poor, wretched, blind;

Sight, riches, healing of the mind,
Yea, all I need in Thee to find,
O Lamb of God, I come, I come.

Just as I am, Thou wilt receive,
Wilt welcome, pardon, cleanse, relieve;
Because Thy promise I believe,
O Lamb of God, I come, I come.

Just as I am, Thy love unknown
Hath broken every barrier down;
Now, to be Thine, yea, Thine alone,
O Lamb of God, I come, I come.

Just as I am, of that free love
The breadth, length, depth, and height to prove,
Here for a season, then above,
O Lamb of God, I come, I come!
(Charlotte Elliott)

- *I am really repenting not because I am caught but eager to change.* I am hiding no longer. Fearing exposure, many run from God. I want to be exposed and set free of hiding my sin, making excuses, and pretending I am righteous. I am so ready and eager to change, right now. I pray this is your attitude.

#2 – Eagerness to Clear Myself
- *I desire to be released from all my past excess baggage.* At the foot of the Cross, lay down all earthly cares and every past sin. Cast your cares on Him for He cares for you.
- *I am eager to be clean.* Some children hate their baths and would go to bed dirty every night and wear yesterday's soiled clothes if their parents would let them. Our Heavenly Father has provided the cleansing blood of Jesus Christ and the washing stream of His Holy Spirit to wash us pure as snow. Let Him clean you up.

- *I am ready to refuse to give the devil a foothold in my life.* Sin crouches at the door of your heart ready to jump into your words or deeds if you don't lock the door and throw away the key. Keep the devil out.
- *I am eager to stop being on the defensive.* A.W. Tozer writes in his booklet, *Five Vows for Spiritual Power,* Christians should never defend themselves. Since God is our sure defense, why would we ever defend ourselves? He writes,

The third vow is this: Never defend yourself. We're all born with a desire to defend ourselves. And if you insist upon defending yourself, God will let you do it. But if you turn the defense of yourself over to God He will defend you. He told Moses once, in Exodus 23:22: "I will be an enemy unto thine enemies and an adversary to thine adversaries."

A long time ago the Lord and I went through the 23rd chapter of Exodus together and He gave it to me. For 30 years now it has been a source of untold blessing to my life. I don't have to fight. The Lord does the fighting for me. And He'll do the same for you. He will be an enemy to your enemy and an adversary to your adversary, and you'll never need to defend yourself.

What do we defend? Well, we defend our service, and particularly we defend our reputation. Your reputation is what people think you are, and if a story gets out about you the big temptation is to try to run it down. But you know, running down the source of a story is a hopeless task. Absolutely hopeless! It's like trying to find the bird after you've found the feather on your lawn. You can't do it. But if you'll turn yourself wholly over to the Lord He will defend you completely and see to it that no one will harm you. 'No weapon that is formed against thee shall prosper.'

He says, and 'every tongue that shall rise against thee in judgment thou shalt condemn' (Isaiah 54:17).

Henry Suso was a great Christian of other days. Once he was seeking what some Christians have told me they are seeking—to know God better. Let's put it like this: you are seeking to have a religious awakening within your spirit that will thrust you farther out into the deep things of God. Well, as Henry Suso was seeking God, people started telling evil stories about the man, and it grieved him so that he wept bitter tears and had great sorrow of heart.

Then one day he looked out the window and saw a dog playing on the lawn. The dog had a mat, and kept picking the mat up, tossing it over his shoulder, running and getting it, tossing it some more, picking it up and tossing it again. God said to Henry Suso, "That mat is your reputation, and I am letting the dogs of sin tear your reputation to shreds and toss it all over the lawn for your own good. One of these days, things will change."

And things did change. It was not very long before people who were tearing his reputation were confounded, and Suso rose into a place that made him a power in his day and a great blessing still to those who sing his hymns and read his works. [3]

- *I am eager to be bold for Christ, not ashamed.* Paul writes, "For I am not ashamed of the gospel, for it is the power of God for salvation to everyone who believes, to the Jew first and also to the Greek. For in it the righteousness of God is revealed from faith to faith; as it is written, "BUT THE RIGHTEOUS man SHALL LIVE BY FAITH" (Romans 1:16-17). There is no shame in repentance. Admit you were wrong and need to be released of your shame, failure, sins, anger, and bitterness.

#3 – Indignation

- *I am disgusted with myself.* Stop being proud. Who cares who sees you cry and weep before God? You are coming in repentance to be seen by God not man. When you become disgusted and desperate, you will repent or you will proudly resist.
- *I desire to crucify the flesh.* Paul writes in Galatians 2:20-21 that he is crucified with Christ. Die to your flesh—your earthly desires and sinful habits.
- *I have a holy revulsion to my wickedness and iniquity.* Yes, you were created in the image of God. Yet, you have done your own thing, gone your own ways, and intentionally transgressed the laws of God. Read of the 10 Commandments for a moment. No one has the power to keep all of them all of the time. Whoever says he does not sin is a liar (1 John 1:10).
- *I am so indignant over my sin that it nauseates me. I want to throw up.* Yes, vomit out the toxin or poison from your being.

#4 – Alarm

- *I fear God.* We have lost the fear of the Lord in churches today. We are no longer alarmed by the vulgar and immoral images on our devices or in our texts. Like Pharaoh, our hearts are hardened toward God. Proverbs 9:10-12 declares, "The fear of the Lord is the beginning of wisdom, And the knowledge of the Holy One is understanding. For by me your days will be multiplied, And years of life will be added to you. If you are wise, you are wise for yourself, And if you scoff, you alone will bear it."
- *I am alarmed by the deceitfulness of my sin.* Your heart should race and your temperature should rise. Get red in face. Blush when you tell a boldfaced lie. Your sin should shock you.

- *I will stop lying to myself and conning myself.* It's time to tell yourself the truth. Yes, you are a sinner and you need to repent and change.
- *I fear spiritual blindness.* You would never drive a car blindfolded. If you did, you would certainly crash, being injured or killed. Why are you navigating through life being spiritually blinded by your selfish pride? Repent. See your way clearly and righteously through life.
- *I am alarmed that my lack of vigilance to repent has kept me from loving God totally.* It's time to love the Lord your God with all your heart, mind, soul, and strength. Jesus Christ is your first and only love. Loving Him totally gives you the power and capacity to love others and yourself.

#5 – Longing

Once you rebuke Satan, Sin, and Worldliness, then you must ask, "***What will be your longing? Your pursuit?***"

- *I am in fiery, passionate pursuit of God.* Preacher and author Tommy Tenney writes, "God Chasers are people whose passion for being in His presence press them to chase the impossible in hopes that the uncatchable might catch them."[4]
- *I so long for God's presence, purity, and holiness.* I have sung the chorus of this song of praise over and over in my quiet times, making these my words, "At Your feet, Lord I bow, Search me and know me, oh God know me now. Take this sin from my heart, I long to be just as you are. I long to be clean. Purify me, Jesus. I long to be holy. Purify me, Jesus. I long to be yours. Purify me, Jesus."

#6 – Concern (Zeal)

- *I have intense zeal for Christ.*
- *I am passionately in love with God.*
- *I am rushing to restore the relationship.*
- *I can't live without Jesus.* Galatians 4:18 reads, "It is fine to be zealous, provided the purpose is good."

In his enduring sermon titled *Christian Zeal*, 19th century Anglican bishop J.C. Ryle wrote:

> "Zeal in Christianity is a burning desire to please God, to do His will, and to advance His glory in the world in every possible way. It is a desire, which is not natural to men or women. It is a desire which the Spirit puts in the heart of every believer when they are converted to Christ, however, a desire which some believers feel so much more strongly than others that they alone deserve to be called "zealous" men and women. This desire is so strong, when it really reigns in a person, that it impels them to make any sacrifice—to go through any trouble—to deny themselves anything—to suffer, to work, to labor, to toil, to spend themselves and be spent, and even to die—if only they can please God and honor Christ. A zealous person in Christianity is preeminently a person of one thing. It is not enough to say that they are earnest, strong, uncompromising, meticulous, wholehearted, and fervent in spirit. They only see one thing, they care for one thing, they live for one thing, they are swallowed up in one thing; and that one thing is to please God."[5]

#7 – Readiness to See Justice Done
- *My repentance leads me to want to make restitution.*
- *I want to make things right with anyone whom I have wronged.*
- *I desire to pay my debts and my vow.*

Insofar as you can make restitution and restore relationship as God leads you, do it. Repentance sets things right with God and man.

Sanctification = Being Release to be Transformed

The Scripture tells us "... elect according to the foreknowledge of God the Father, in **sanctification** of the Spirit, for obedience and sprinkling of the blood of Jesus Christ" (1 Peter 1:2 NKJV, emphasis mine) and, "Now may the God of peace Himself *sanctify you entirely*; and may your spirit and soul and body be preserved complete, without blame at the coming of our Lord Jesus Christ. *Faithful is He who calls you*, and *He also will bring it to pass.*" (1Thessalonians 5:23-24, emphasis mine).

Transformation according to Romans 12:1-2 is offering ourselves as living sacrifices; being transformed by the renewing of our minds. When Hannah came before God, she sought the mind of God. She cried out for justice, mercy, and grace. When we repent, our renewed mind—the mind of Christ—doesn't meditate on things below but on things above. The renewed mind thinks this way:

> *Finally, brethren, whatever is true, whatever is honorable, whatever is right, whatever is pure, whatever is lovely, whatever is of good repute, if there is any excellence and if anything worthy of praise, dwell on these things. The things you have learned and received and heard and seen in me, practice these things, and the God of peace will be with you.* (Philippians 4:8-9)

❧

**After the release of repentance,
we can receive the righteousness of Christ,
for He is our Righteousness.**

❧

Has your repentance been real? Then examine yourself. Examine your actions, thoughts, and feelings. Are they ...

- True—honest, real, and trustworthy?

76

- Honorable—glorifying and honoring God not self or man?
- Right—righteous, holy, and pure?
- Lovely—loving, kind, and selfless?
- Of good repute—the reputation of Christ is at stake not yours? Humility, not pride, marks you.
- Excellent—God's best and highest. As author Oswald Chambers said in the title of his 1992 devotional classic: *Your Utmost for His Highest (Discovery House: 1992).*
- Worthy of praise—do your good works rooted in good motivations bring glory and praise to your Heavenly Father?

If so, you will receive what Hannah received and Paul wrote about, "The God of peace will be with you."

Examine Yourself

We must get to the root if release is to happen, and we are to receive God's peace. Eradicate the root of wrong, anger, sin, and bitterness in your life. Really repent. Godly sorrow such as Hannah's brought to her a new root of righteousness, holiness, and peace in her life. The same will be true for you. Read how Paul wraps us his instructions about godly sorrow:

> *"Therefore whoever eats the bread or drinks the cup of the Lord in an unworthy manner, shall be guilty of the body and the blood of the Lord. But a man must examine himself, and in so doing he is to eat of the bread and drink of the cup. For he who eats and drinks, eats and drinks judgment to himself if he does not judge the body rightly. For this reason many among you are weak and sick, and a number sleep."* (1 Corinthians 11:27-30)

I invite you right now to:
- **REPENT & GET OVER IT**: your past hurts, sins, failures, pain, fears, uncertainties, doubts and mistakes.
- Turn away from your wrong and sinful habits.
- Turn to Jesus Christ and ask forgiveness.

- Start following Jesus. (Acts 2:38; 2 Corinthians 7:10-12; Mt. 16:24; 1 John 1:9)

Repentance Opens the Door to Transformation:
- From Fragmentation to Transformation
- The Divine Process and Work of the Spirit in Us is Sanctification

This is God's End Game for You

God's *"telos—be perfect* even as your Father in heaven is perfect"—or God's will (desire, destiny) for you is to be "conformed to the image of Christ Jesus" which is to be "like Him."

Fragmentation—Original sin is separation from God which tore you away from the image of God and shattered your God-image into a broken, sin-infected self-image.

Transformation is, "That no flesh should glory in His presence. But of Him you are in Christ Jesus, who became for us wisdom from God—and righteousness and *sanctification* and redemption—that, as it is written, *"He who glories, let him glory in the Lord"* (1 Corinthians 1:29-31, NKJV, emphasis mine).

"For this is the will of God, your **sanctification**." (1 Thessalonians 4:3, emphasis mine)

Sanctification – Be Holy as God is Holy, Like Christ—*The Holy & Anointed One.*

"That each of you should know how to possess his own vessel in *sanctification* and honor, not in passion of lust, like the Gentiles who do not know God" (1 Thessalonians 4:4-6) and, "...because God has chosen you from the beginning for salvation through sanctification by the Spirit and faith in the truth." (2 Thessalonians 2:13).

How does transformation happen? It's a process of spiritual growth and maturing that Paul writes about in Romans 5:1-5, "Therefore, having been justified by faith, we have peace with God through our Lord Jesus Christ, through whom also we have obtained our introduction by faith into this grace in which we stand; and [b]we exult in hope of the glory of God. And not only this, but we also exult in our tribulations, knowing that tribulation brings about perseverance; and perseverance, proven character; and proven character, hope; and hope does not disappoint, because the love of God has been poured out within our hearts through the Holy Spirit who was given to us."

So, our Character/Identity is changed or transformed into the image and likeness of Christ. Declare these promises for your transformation:

- "And as we have borne the *image* of the *man of dust, we shall also bear the image of the heavenly Man*" (1 Corinthians 15:49) and, "And we, who with unveiled faces all reflect the Lord's glory, are being *transformed* into his *likeness* with ever-increasing glory, which comes from the Lord, who is the Spirit" (2 Corinthians 3:18).

- Finally, what do we ultimately receive from God and what are we released to do? *Love.* We recognize Christ in ourselves and others by God's love. Imprint these words from Christ on your mind and heart: "You did not choose Me but I chose you, and appointed you that you would go and bear fruit, and that your fruit would remain, so that whatever you ask of the Father in My name He may give to you. This I command you, *that you love one another.*" (John 15:16-17).

   "For as many of you as were baptized into Christ have *put on* Christ" (Galatians 3:27).

   "But the *fruit* of the Spirit is love, joy, peace, patience, kindness, goodness, faithfulness, gentleness and self-control (Galatians 5:22-23).

You are released to receive the likeness and image of Christ!

Ask yourself ...
- *Whose image or likeness do you bear or reflect?*
- *In whom is your self-image rooted?*

- *From whom or what do you receive your identity?*
- *What birthmark identifies you?*

Let this be your prayer ...

"May Christ increase as I decrease." (John 3:30)

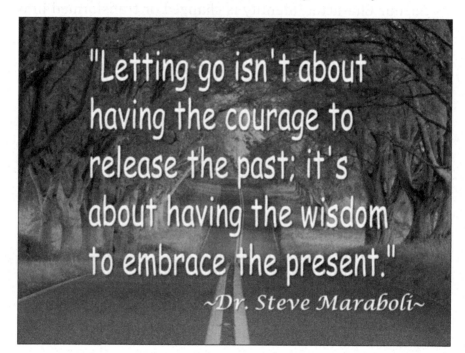

"Letting go isn't about having the courage to release the past; it's about having the wisdom to embrace the present."
~Dr. Steve Maraboli~

Chapter 7

But God

She [Hannah] made a vow and said, "O Lord of hosts, if You will indeed look on the affliction of Your maidservant and remember me, and not forget Your maidservant, but will give Your maidservant a son, then I will give him to the Lord all the days of his life, and a razor shall never come on his head." (1 Samuel 1:11)

All of us have issues; some of those issues arose in our childhood. Others go deeply into our past for generations. If you never go back to the issues, if you never go back to where a curse or an affliction started, you will not be able to be able to release the past or receive your breakthrough for where God is leading you.

All of us are a byproduct of our past, but what we need to do as a part of releasing and receiving is to put a comma after our past, and then say "but God."

It's an English lesson. For example, you can say:

I used to be this way, *but God*;

I used to be a whoremonger, *but God*;

I used to be on drugs, *but God* ...

I used to be able to cuss you out like sailor, *but God*...

I used to do some crazy stuff,

I used to shoot folks,
    I used to deal in drugs,
      I used to be a drug dealer,
    I used to be a pimp,
      I used to do all sorts of bad things, *but God ...*
I used to give people my time that did not deserve my time, *but God ...*
      I used to be in bad or ungodly relationships, *but God ...*

What we've got to do is to get to a point that we get to the comma and the "but God" as we journey through life. Hannah's prayer to God includes a "but God." It went something like this, "My life has been filled with misery, but God ...You can change all that by giving me a son whom I will give back to You."

When we release, then we can receive whatever God wills for us to have, do, and receive. A hand holding tightly to the past cannot receive the future. Yes, Hannah could have kept grieving, being angry and bitter, and ultimately could never have received anything new from God. She knew God had designed her as a wife to be fruitful and have children. Her "but God" was simply this, "I may be barren, *but God* can give me a son."

God Can Change Everything When We Release and Receive

When we release our assumptions and preconceived notions, God can change our minds. When we release negative emotions like sadness, anger, fear, or bitterness, God can change our feelings. And, when we release past sins, failures, and transgressions, God can change our eternal destination. For example:

I *thought* miracles were only for the people in the Bible, *but God* healed me ... and changed my mind.

I *felt* abandoned, hopeless, and without a dream, *but God* gave me a vision of my future in Christ.

I was *lost* in my sin and failures, *but God* forgave me and made me clean and whole.

Amazing Grace, how sweet the sound,
That saved a wretch like me.

*I once was lost **but now** I'm found,*
*Was blind, **but now** I see.*

For the next few pages, I will share with you some "but God" stories in the Bible that can immediately apply to your life right now.

Childless, *But God*

We have been exploring Hannah's story of being barren and God changing everything by giving her Samuel. However, the most astounding Bible story about being childless, *but God,* can be found in the Bible's Book of Beginnings—Genesis:

> *Then God said to Abraham, "As for Sarai your wife, you shall not call her name Sarai, but Sarah shall be her name. "I will bless her, and indeed I will give you a son by her. Then I will bless her, and she shall be a mother of nations; kings of peoples will come from her." Then Abraham fell on his face and laughed, and said in his heart, "Will a child be born to a man one hundred years old? And will Sarah, who is ninety years old, bear a child?"*
>
> *And Abraham said to God, "Oh that Ishmael might live before You!"*
>
> ***But God** said, "No, but Sarah your wife will bear you a son, and you shall call his name Isaac; and I will establish My covenant with him for an everlasting covenant for his descendants after him.* (Genesis 17:15-19)

Abraham and Sara were old and childless ... well past the child-bearing years. *But God* had a plan that went beyond human limitations. They were powerless, *but God* is all-powerful, omnipotent.

Over the years, I have seen many couples believe that they couldn't have children. *But God* intervened. Some adopted children; soon after the adoption, they got pregnant. God was in the adoption, *but God* was also in the conception.

I've seen a businessman entrepreneur lose his shirt and even his money and home in bankruptcy followed by foreclosure. All his colleagues, family, and friends thought he was washed up and finished. *But God* gave him a new product or service, angel investors, and a comeback that only God could have engineered.

What is the *but God* intervention that you need in your life? Are you in lack? Do you need to release a spirit of poverty? Yes, you are temporarily out of cash, *but God* has made you rich in Christ. Paul writes, "For you know the grace of our Lord Jesus Christ, that though He was rich, yet for your sake He became poor, so that you through His poverty might become rich" (2 Corinthians 8:9).

You may feel abandoned by a spouse through divorce, or unloved by an absentee parent. *But God* sets the solitary in families and adopts us who are orphans making us His children (Psalm 68:6; Romans 8).

Joseph was sold into slavery by his brothers, who later had to come to him to beg for food. Joseph said, "Now, therefore, it was not you who sent me here [to Egypt], *but God*; and He has made me a father to Pharaoh and lord of all his household and ruler over the land of Egypt" (Genesis 45:8, emphasis mine). Joseph had dreams that seemed impossible for a nomadic child to achieve. His brothers hated him for his dreams, threw him into a pit, and sold him into slavery. Then Joseph's Egyptian master, Potiphar, threw him into prison when Potiphar's wife accused Joseph of making sexual advances toward her. Joseph's dreams were impossible, *but God* turned what man had intended for evil into good.

Genesis 50:19-21 reads, "Joseph said to them, 'Do not be afraid, for am I in the place of God? But as for you, you meant evil against me; *but God* meant it for good, in order to bring it about as it is this day, to save many people alive. Now therefore, do not be afraid; I will provide for you and your little ones.' And he comforted them and spoke kindly to them."

When All Hope Seems to Vanish, *But God*

Just remember some of the *but God* instances in the Scriptures.

- The walls of Jericho were impenetrable, *but God* brought those walls tumbling down.
- The strength of Samson was completely gone after Delilah cut his hair, *but God* gave him strength to pull down the whole temple of the Philistines who worshipped idols.
- The Philistine giant name Goliath was unbeatable, *but God* gave a shepherd boy named David a sharpshooter's aim with a sling shot killing Goliath with a single stone.
- The army of Sennacherib, the Assyrian king, had a death grip siege around Jerusalem, *but God* sent an angel of death into the enemy's camp and killed 185,000 soldiers while Sennacherib's own sons assassinated him back in Nineveh.
- The tiny nation of Israel was conquered by mighty Rome and hopelessly mired in a legalistic, lifeless religion. They ran after false messiahs and prophets, *but God* sent a baby to an unwed Jewish virgin—poor, unknown, and from Nazareth—a nowhere kind of town. That baby Jesus was the true Messiah who would save the world.

Oh yes, remember that it was Passover Friday, and that baby boy became a man named Yeshua and now hung on a cross. His friends and all but one of his disciples had deserted him. It appeared that all hope was lost on that black Friday, *but God* had a plan on that coming Sunday. He raised the crucified King of the Jews from the dead. *But God* turned what the devil had thought was a victory into a stunning defeat of sin and death. Pastor Tony Campolo's classic sermon, *It's Friday But Sunday's Coming*, proclaims the riveting *But God* paradox of the cross. Yes, it was Friday and the devil thought he had won. Jesus was nailed to a cross, bleeding and dying.

All hope seemed lost on that Friday as Jesus was crucified, dead, and buried, *but God.* It wasn't all over. As dawn faintly lit the eastern sky over Jerusalem, a tomb sealed and guarded by Roman soldiers suddenly had its stone rolled away. In one moment before dawn, the night enshrouded a dead Jesus; *but God* at first light in a twinkling of an eye raised Jesus from the dead! Hallelujah. He is Risen!

So it shall be on that glorious day when Jesus returns for us. Believers who died in Christ hear the trumpet sound and suddenly, *but God* raises all those who believed upon the name of Jesus from the dead. You may die before Christ returns, but as a believer in Jesus Christ as Lord and Savior, take comfort in these words:

> "*For this we say to you by the word of the Lord, that we who are alive and remain until the coming of the Lord, will not precede those who have fallen asleep. For the Lord Himself will descend from heaven with a shout, with the voice of the archangel and with the trumpet of God, and the dead in Christ will rise first. Then we who are alive and remain will be caught up together with them in the clouds to meet the Lord in the air, and so we shall always be with the Lord. Therefore comfort one another with these words.*" (1 Thessalonians 4:15-18)

Your loved one who died from cancer, heart disease, diabetes, in a fatal accident or in a war, is now absent from the body but present with the Lord. The wages of sin and living in this world are death, *but God* gives us the victory over sin and death through Jesus Christ. Read the following words out loud, and loudly so that your ears hear the truth, for faith comes by hearing and hearing by the word of God:

> *For one will hardly die for a righteous man; though perhaps for the good man someone would dare even to die.* **But God** *demonstrates His own love toward us, in that while we were yet sinners, Christ died for us. Much more then, having now been justified by His blood, we shall be saved from the wrath of God through Him. For if while we were enemies we*

were reconciled to God through the death of His Son, much more, having been reconciled, we shall be saved by His life. And not only this, but we also exult in God through our Lord Jesus Christ, through whom we have now received the reconciliation. (Romans 5:7-11)

The New Testament abounds in the "but God" paradoxes of what the world has in store for us *but God* changes everything, turning the world upside down. There is bad news in the world, *but God in Christ* showers us with grace and good news. Declare these truths for your release and receive God's promises for you:

- They crucified Christ and laid Him in a tomb, *"but God* raised Him from the dead."
- We are chosen to proclaim the wisdom of God; we are considered fools in the world, *"but God* has chosen the foolish things of the world to shame the wise, and God has chosen the weak things of the world to shame the things which are strong, and the base things of the world and the despised God has chosen, the things that are not, so that He may nullify the things that are, so that no man may boast before God. *But by His doing* you are in Christ Jesus, who became to us wisdom from God, and righteousness and sanctification, and redemption, so that, just as it is written, "'LET HIM WHO BOASTS, BOAST IN THE LORD'" (1 Corinthians 1:27-31).
- We may plant, others may water, *"But God* brings the increase" (1 Corinthians 3:6).
- The world may cause us to fight with one another, *"but God* has called us to peace" (1 Corinthians 7:15).
- We find ourselves afflicted on every side, "conflicts without, fears within. *But God,* who comforts the depressed, comforted us..." (2 Corinthians 7:6).
- We have earned the wrath of God for our sins and rebellion, *"But God,* being rich in mercy, because of His great love for us with which He loved us, even when we were dead in our transgressions, made us alive together with

Christ (for grace have you been saved), and raised us up with Him, and seated us with Him in heavenly places in Christ Jesus" (Ephesians 2:4-6).

When sorrows engulf you as they did Hannah, get to the anointing, declare your release, let go of the past and receive the promises of God. As the world and the enemy rejoices over your momentary afflictions and temporary losses, take heart and boldly declare,

But God is able to supply all my needs,
To snatch victory out of the jaws of defeat,
And to save me to the uttermost.
BUT GOD!
Amen.

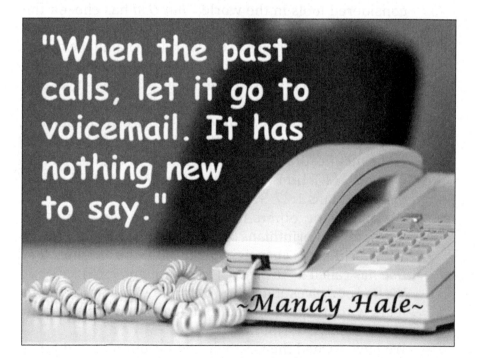

"When the past calls, let it go to voicemail. It has nothing new to say."

~Mandy Hale~

Chapter 8

The Expiration Date

*Then Eli answered and said, "Go in peace; and
may the God of Israel grant your petition that you
have asked of Him." She said, "Let your maidservant find favor in your sight." So the woman went
her way and ate, and her face was no longer sad.*
(1 Samuel 1:17-18)

*There is an appointed time for everything. And there
is a time for every event under heaven —*
A time to give birth and a time to die;
A time to plant and a time to uproot what is planted.
A time to kill and a time to heal;
A time to tear down and a time to build up.
A time to weep and a time to laugh;
A time to mourn and a time to dance.
(Ecclesiastes 3:1-4)

U nderstand that life has seasons. Ecclesiastes 3:1 says, "To
everything there is a season." This means that if everything
has a season, then there is an expiration date associated with that
season. Yes, there was a beginning to the troubles; but, there's an
end in sight as well. There is an expiration date to the stuff we've
been dealing with. Any time milk goes beyond its expiration date

it spoils, it begins to sour, and it begins to look bad, smell bad, and taste bad. Any time you go beyond your expiration date with the stuff you've been dealing with it begins to spoil, it begins to stink, and you begin to sour because you've gone beyond the expiration date.

So, if we're dealing with bitterness and it's gone beyond its expiration date, the bitterness sours, spoils, and begins to spoil the inside of us. Then that spoilage affects how we speak, it affects our hearts, it affects the way we see people, and it affects the way we see ourselves because that issue has gone beyond its expiration date inside of us.

Anger can go beyond its expiration date. Sometimes we've been mad at that person for too long. The bitterness, the foolishness, the aggravation, the wrath, the resentment, the adversity, the tribulations, and the depression has gone way beyond their expiration date. It's time for us to release in order to be able to receive what God has in store for each and every one of us.

The Past Has Expired, Release It!

The word *season* is from the Hebrew word *zaman*. It means "an appointed or an affixed time." If everything has a season, then everything you go through in life is appointed by God. Each season is fixed by God for a duration so that you will get what you need in that season, not only to produce a harvest or to reap the harvest that's there, but also to sow for the harvest that's going to come. Every moment of your life involves two things: *sowing and reaping.*

There is a harvest in your life right now. There is a person who works in your office who is ready to be harvested. God has sent multiple words to him and a plethora of messages to prepare him for the moment of your divine appointment—so that when he says, "My God, I just don't know what to do," then *you* know what to do. You know what to say because the divine appointment is part of God's purpose, and you are one who reaps the harvest.

It was time for a divine appointment in Hannah's season. She had a divine appointment with God. Life is all about a season in your life producing all that God wants out of it before you get to the next one. Don't try to get out of a season. Find out when and how to meet with God and keep His divine appointments for your present season. Hannah knew that she had to get with God in her season. Her purpose was to be fruitful and multiply. She wanted a harvest from her sowing in tears. The Scriptures declare,

> *Those who sow in tears shall reap with joyful shouting. He who goes to and fro weeping, carrying his bag of seed, Shall indeed come again with a shout of joy, bringing his sheaves with him.* (Psalm 126:5-6)

Hannah had spent much of her married season in life sowing in tears. Weeping before her husband or her husband's other wife did produce what she needed. She had to get to the anointing. She took her bag full of tears, her petitions, to the Lord. She had a divine appointment with God.

Understand what I am sharing with you: A season is about divine appointments, and it's not about you. It's about those around you whom God wants to touch through you. He cannot get that harvest without you. Hannah sensed that her season and divine appointment with God wasn't about what she wanted; it was all about what God wanted. He wanted to meet with her and assure her that the child she was to receive wasn't just her blessing. The child would be a blessing to others; in fact, the coming child names Samuel would judge a nation, anoint Israel's first two kings, and prophetically declare the coming Hebrew Messiah (Anointed One) who would save the world.

What if Hannah had stayed home during the feast and sulked? What if she had been so bound up in self-pity that she was paralyzed in the past season of her life and unwilling to keep the divine appointment God was setting for her? What if she had never sown in tears? Then a season of joyful shouting would never have arrived for her or for her nation.

❧

Seasons are filled with opportunities and divine appointments.
They come and go. They will expire.
Don't miss them. Keep divine appointments.
Seize the opportunities God puts in front of you.
The time to maximize them is now.
Stop procrastinating.

❧

Your season is filled with divine appointments. They are set times for God to speak into your life through others that you encounter. God used Eli to speak into Hannah's life during her divine appointment in the Tabernacle. Her season of barrenness and being unfruitful was about to expire, but she would never have known that if she had missed her divine appointment with God.

Release the tears, pain, and sorrow you have experienced in this season. Don't get stuck in the wilderness. Israel missed her divine appointment to enter into the Promised Land and had to wander in the wilderness for 40 years. Stop wandering, wondering, and wishing for a new season. Keep divine appointments now with God and with others that He brings to you to speak His words of wisdom, counsel, hope, and newness.

God spoke a new thing into Hannah's life. He can and will do the same for you. In this season of sowing in tears, God is saying to you:

"Behold, I will do something new,
Now it will spring forth;
Will you not be aware of it?
I will even make a roadway in the wilderness,
Rivers in the desert." (Isaiah 43:19)

You are on the threshold of a new season in your life. Release the old. Its time has expired. The harvest is over. The fruit is no longer on the vine. You have finished sowing in tears. Joy comes in the morning!

The New Season Has Arrived, Receive It!

The next thing we must understand about this process is time. *To everything there is a season, a **time** ...*

A *time* and a *season*—in Hebrew, these words are almost synonymous. But there is enough of a difference between them to understand the combination of the two words together.

Time is an opportunity. In fact, time is a container filled with limitless opportunities given to you by a God of abundance, not lack. He has plans for you. The plans of the diligent will prosper. Even if you fail at the first plan, by His grace, He will give you more. Fail once, and another plan comes from God. Fail a dozen times, He gives you still another good plan. Fail more than 6,000 times, as Thomas Edison did in his quest for a filament to work in a light bulb, and God will give you Plan Number 6001 that will work if you don't quit.

❧

> **When you are walking in God's season,**
> **faithfully trying His plans not yours,**
> **Keeping His divine appointments,**
> **and doing what He desires,**
> **You can't fail unless...you quit!**

❧

It is a proper time. In other words, a season is a fixed, appointed time of opportunity that God is putting in front of you, and the only time in history that opportunity will occur for you is in that season. But if you are only focused on the season instead of the appointment, you will miss what God wants to do. Remember these promises:

Commit your way to the Lord,
Trust also in Him, and He will do it.
He will bring forth your righteousness as the light
And your judgment as the noonday.

Rest in the Lord and wait patiently for Him;
Do not fret because of him who prospers in his way,
Because of the man who carries out wicked schemes.
(Psalm 37:5-7)

Commit your works to the Lord
And your plans will be established.
(Psalm 16:3)

Yes, when your plans are from the Lord, keep on trusting Him because the only way you can ultimately fail is if you quit!

You may be looking around and saying, "I hate winter, and I hate dry seasons." While you are looking around and fighting God over the season that He has put you in, all of these opportunities and appointments are zooming by you. Eternity is being lost because you are not focusing on the divine presence where God has you right now. Know that when you go through a season, the Christian walk is a step at a time, and *now* is the important time. Now. Right now.

You may be rushing through life to get to tomorrow, but Jesus says, "Don't even think about tomorrow. Today has got enough for you to be concerned about" (Read Matthew 6). There is a moment, an appointment, an opportunity for God to be pleased. This divine appointment is not about you. It's about the person that He has put before you. It is about the new business proposition confronting you. It is about the opportunity to move somewhere, to experience something new, for the old is passing away. Those people in your life—the ones who have decided that you are going to live in one place or just do one thing—might want to check with God. He may need you to move out of your rut and routine, down a road you've never been, into a job or relationship that is risky, and obey Him no matter what.

*And it shall be that if you earnestly **obey** My commandments which I command you today, to **love** the LORD your God and **serve** Him with all your heart and with all your soul, then I will **give** you the rain for your **land** in its **season**, the early rain and the latter rain, that you may gather in your grain, your new wine, and your oil.* (Deuteronomy 11:13-14 NKJV)

Keep Divine Appointments

You are special to God. The hairs on your head are numbered by him. He called and formed you in the womb. In reading Hannah's story, we know that God had a special plan for Samuel, the child given not only to Hannah but also to a nation with a calling of judge and prophet on his life. Read Psalm 139:1-16 (MSG) as it applies to Hannah, to Samuel, and to you:

God, investigate my life; get all the facts firsthand.
I'm an open book to you; even from a distance, you know what I'm thinking.

You know when I leave and when I get back;
I'm never out of your sight

You know everything I'm going to say before I start the first sentence.
I look behind me and you're there, then up ahead and you're there, too —your reassuring presence, coming and going.
This is too much, too wonderful — I can't take it all in!

Is there anyplace I can go to avoid your Spirit? to be out of your sight?
If I climb to the sky, you're there! If I go underground, you're there!
If I flew on morning's wings to the far western horizon,
You'd find me in a minute — you're already there waiting!
Then I said to myself, "Oh, he even sees me in the dark! At night I'm immersed in the light!" It's a fact: darkness isn't dark to you; night and day, darkness and light, they're all the same to you.

Oh yes, you shaped me first inside, then out; you formed me in my mother's womb.
I thank you, High God — you're breathtaking! Body and soul, I am marvelously made!
I worship in adoration — what a creation!
You know me inside and out, you know every bone in my body;
You know exactly how I was made, bit by bit, how I was sculpted from nothing into something.
Like an open book, you watched me grow from conception to birth;
all the stages of my life were spread out before you,
The days of my life all prepared before I'd even lived one day.

God created you with His purpose for you in mind. The Hebrew word for "purpose" is "chephets" The same word is translated as "desires" in Psalm 37:4, "Delight yourself in the Lord; And He will give you the desires of your heart." Those desires were imparted to you when He formed you in the womb. Interestingly, the word "de-sire" is formed of two words "of the father." In other words, the desires in your heart were placed there by the Father. When you surrender all that you are to Him, when your every want become His every wish, when your will is fully transformed by His will, then the desires of your heart are His will and way for you, i.e. your purpose in life.

Every season in your life as a believer flows like a river in the desert through the dry and parched places. Notice I said, "through." Nothing can stop you from going with God, being a sailboat catching the wind of His Spirit flowing with the river of God. Nothing could have kept Hannah from her divine appointment with God on that day of destiny when she poured out her tears and heartfelt desires to the Lord in the Tabernacle. She got to the place of the anointing ready to release all that was old and embrace all the "new" that God wanted to birth in her. She released all her past pain, hurt, and sorrow. Her tears flowed for the now, but the next thing God had for her—the new season He would have her step into—would birth blessing for her household and the entire household of God. Amazing!

Keep sowing in tears; you will be shouting with joy. Continue to release the past in order to receive God's future for you. Stay in His Presence. Keep divine appointments. Your harvest this season is only preparation for the next season's sowing and harvest. Now you may only be experiencing thirtyfold, but sixtyfold is coming, and a hundredfold harvest is promised.

Are you willing to release the past and step into a new season?

Will you be prepared to receive? What you receive will be more than enough!

Put your dancing shoes on...Declare God's decree:

Young women will dance and be happy,
young men and old men will join in.
I'll convert their weeping into laughter,
lavishing comfort, invading their grief with joy.
I'll make sure that their priests get three square meals a day
*and that my people have **more than enough**.*
God's Decree.
(Jeremiah 31:13-14 MSG)

Final Word

Hannah released, Hannah received, but before Hannah released and received, she rejoiced.

> *And they rose up [you've got to get up] in the morning early, and worshipped*
> *before the Lord, [after one releases and before one receives, one must rejoice]*
> *and retuned, and came to their house to Ramah: and Elkanah knew Hannah his wife;*
> *and the Lord remembered her.*
> (1 Samuel 1:19)

This is an advance praise. After I release something and before I receive, I'm going to start praising Him. I rejoice before I get to receive. I just stand and praise Him. So after I release and before I receive, I can give Him advance praise because I know it is coming. Some of us want to receive something, but we haven't gotten to the point when we're ready to release our old ways. You know in your spirit that you have released and you're going to be able to receive everything God has for you. As I challenge you to release something, I challenge you to rejoice right where you are and I believe in my heart that you will be able to receive what God has in store for your life.

I stand today, able to say that in the midst of waiting, you must give Him praise. While awaiting what God has in store, give him what He deserves. Praise Him like you have lost your mind—because I know that God is a mighty God who is willing to work out everything on your behalf. I know that God is willing to give us everything once we give Him what is due Him.

There's a miracle with your name on it. There's a blessing with your name on it. There's a breakthrough with your name on it. He's waiting for you to give him praise. He's waiting for you to get outside of the norm. Stop doing what you've been doing, get up off your behind, and give Him what is due Him because He's worthy of all the praise.

You must be willing to release, praise Him, worship Him, rejoice, and then be able to receive. If you've got bitterness, anger, and all this stuff built up inside of you because somebody did something to you 10 or 15 years ago or five days ago, release it and be able to receive everything that God has in store for your life. It will **not** come until you release.

Some of us have been full of anger, bitterness, and hatefulness for years, but today the expiration date has come for you to release it so you can receive what God has for your life.

Come Into His Presence Rejoicing

Stop complaining. Sow your tears so you may reap in joy. Hannah got up and rejoiced before God. Yes, she had her issues, problems at home, and trials in life. Nonetheless, she worshipped, praised God, and came into His Presence. There may have been tears in her eyes, but there was praise on her lips. Instead of complaining that you have not yet seen the promises of God fulfilled in your life, you can thank God for all He has done and will do.

God has saved you, is saving you, and will save you.
> **God has delivered you, is delivering you, and will deliver you.**
> > **God by the stripes of Christ has healed you, is healing you, and will heal you.**

Your Heavenly Father is God of the now, the new, and the next. Now it's time to rejoice, praise, and be thankful to Him for all He has done. Rejoice in the new thing He's about to do. Be thankfully obedient to the next thing He asks you to do. Keep sowing for in due season you will reap an abundant harvest. Hannah did ... and so will you!

Let Psalm 98:4 be your declaration: "Shout joyfully to the Lord, all the earth; Break forth in song, rejoice and sing praises." Paul writes in Philippians 4:4. "Rejoice in the Lord always. Again I say, Rejoice!"

Prayerfully consider today the things in your life that you need to release in order to receive everything that God has in store for your life. Please remember this final thought: If you don't release the bitterness, negativity, ungodliness, and foolishness that has filled your past, you will not have room to receive the love, peace, joy, godly direction and promises that God has in store for our lives. Release To Receive!

On the following pages you will find a prayer declaration journal for you to use over the next month.

30 Days of Releasing to Receive the Promises of God

I encourage you to make a commitment to Christ. Ask another prayer partner to agree to do this with you. The word "impartation" describes the means by which God imparts his anointing. After the first 30 days of making your prayer declarations, I urge you to do it again for at least another two months so that you receive a powerful impartation in your personal life, relationships, in your work and service at church and in your community outreach as well.

Advance praise happens when rejoicing is continually in our hearts, thankfulness permeates our every thought, and praise is continually on our lips. Release the past to receive praise for everything, at all times. We are giving thanks in everything as we release to receive.

Enter into His gates with thanksgiving,
And into His courts with praise.
Be thankful to Him,
And bless His name.
(Psalm 100:4)
Thank God that you are *released to receive!*

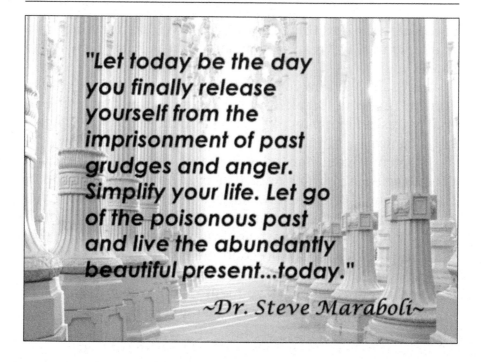

"Let today be the day
you finally release
yourself from the
imprisonment of past
grudges and anger.
Simplify your life. Let go
of the poisonous past
and live the abundantly
beautiful present...today."

~Dr. Steve Maraboli~

30 DAYS OF RELEASING TO RECEIVE THE PROMISES OF GOD

Day 1

Release the Old – Receive the New

Declare this three times a day and three times each time you declare it based on Isaiah 43:

**In the Name of Jesus Christ, I release my dwelling on the past, and receive every new thing that God has for me through His abundant grace.
Amen.**

Forget the former things;
do not dwell on the past.

See, I am doing a new thing!
Now it springs up; do you not perceive it?
I am making a way in the desert
and streams in the wasteland.
(Isaiah 43:18-19 NIV)

Write down what God speaks to you through the Scriptures and by the Holy Spirit:

_____

_____

_____

_____

_____

_____

Write down a prayer of advance praise for what God is and will be doing in and through you as you release and receive.

_____

_____

_____

_____

_____

_____

_____

_____

Memorize the above Scripture passage. Write the declaration and Scripture passage on a card to carry on your person or put it into your smart phone as a note or voice message. Read or hear it and declare it once an hour throughout the day. *Meditate on God's Truth this way day and night.*

Day 2

Release Habitual Sin – Receive Abundant Mercy

Declare this based on Romans 6:

In the Name of Jesus Christ, I confess and release every sin habit, I resist the device of the devil, and I receive His abundant mercy and grace.
Amen.

What shall we say then? Shall we continue in sin, that grace may abound? God forbid. We who died to sin, how shall we any longer live therein? Or are ye ignorant that all we who were baptized into Christ Jesus were baptized into his death? We were buried therefore with him through baptism unto death: that like as Christ was raised from the dead through the glory of the Father, so we also might walk in newness of life. (Romans 6:1-4)

Write down what God speaks to you through the Scriptures and by the Holy Spirit:

_____

_____

_____

_____

_____

_____

Write down a prayer of advance praise for what God is and will be doing in and through you as you release and receive.

_____

_____

_____

_____

_____

_____

_____

_____

Memorize the above Scripture passage. Write the declaration and Scripture passage on a card to carry on your person or put it into your smart phone as a note or voice message. Read or hear it and declare it once an hour throughout the day. *Meditate on God's Truth this way day and night.*

Day 3

Release Sin – Receive Forgiveness

Declare this based on 1 John 1:

**In the Name of Jesus Christ, I confess and release all my past sins and transgressions to Him, I receive the cleansing forgiveness of the blood of Christ, I declare
I am a forgiven child of God.
Amen.**

If we confess our sin he is faithful and righteous to forgive us our sins, and to cleanse us from all unrighteousness. 1 John 1:9

Write down what God speaks to you through the Scriptures and by the Holy Spirit:

_____

_____

_____

_____

_____

_____

_____

_____

Write down a prayer of advance praise for what God is and will be doing in and through you as you release and receive.

_____

_____

_____

_____

_____

_____

_____

_____

Memorize the above Scripture passage. Write the declaration and Scripture passage on a card to carry on your person or put it into your smart phone as a note or voice message. Read or hear it and declare it once an hour throughout the day. *Meditate on God's Truth this way day and night.*

Day 4

Release Procrastination – Receive Patient Perseverance

Declare this based on James 4:

**In the Name of Jesus Christ, I release and cut off my procrastination, I receive the patience and perseverance of the Holy Spirit To do all the good works
God has assigned to me.
Amen.**

"Therefore, to one who knows the right thing to do
and does not do it, to him it is sin." (James 4:17)

Write down what God speaks to you through the Scriptures and by the Holy Spirit:

_____

_____

_____

_____

_____

_____

_____

_____

Write down a prayer of advance praise for what God is and will be doing in and through you as you release and receive.

_____

_____

_____

_____

_____

_____

_____

_____

Memorize the above Scripture passage. Write the declaration and Scripture passage on a card to carry on your person or put it into your smart phone as a note or voice message. Read or hear it and declare it once an hour throughout the day. *Meditate on God's Truth this way day and night.*

Day 5

Release Weakness – Receive Power

Declare this based on Joshua 1:

**In the Name of Jesus Christ,
I release fear, weakness, and discouragement.
I receive God's power, love, and the mind of Christ.
God is with me every step of the way!
Amen.**

*Strength! Courage!
Don't be timid;
Don't get discouraged.
God, your God, is with you every step you take!*
(Joshua 1:9 MSG)

Write down what God speaks to you through the Scriptures and by the Holy Spirit:

_____

_____

_____

_____

_____

_____

_____

_____

Write down a prayer of advance praise for what God is and will be doing in and through you as you release and receive.

_____

_____

_____

_____

_____

_____

_____

_____

Memorize the above Scripture passage. Write the declaration and Scripture passage on a card to carry on your person or put it into your smart phone as a note or voice message. Read or hear it and declare it once an hour throughout the day. *Meditate on God's Truth this way day and night.*

Day 6

Release Lack – Receive the Prize

Declare this based on Philippians 3:

**In the name of Jesus Christ,
I release my lack of passion, motivation, and initiative.
I receive the prize of the high calling of God.
Amen.**

*I press toward the mark for the prize of the high
calling of God in Christ Jesus.* (Philippians 3:14)

Write down what God speaks to you through the Scriptures
and by the Holy Spirit:

_____

_____

_____

_____

_____

_____

_____

_____

Write down a prayer of advance praise for what God is and will be doing in and through you as you release and receive.

_____

_____

_____

_____

_____

_____

_____

_____

Memorize the above Scripture passage. Write the declaration and Scripture passage on a card to carry on your person or put it into your smart phone as a note or voice message. Read or hear it and declare it once an hour throughout the day. *Meditate on God's Truth this way day and night.*

Day 7

Release Unforgiveness – Receive Mercy and Grace

Declare this based on Luke 17:

**In the Name of Jesus Christ,
I release all offenses and unforgiveness in my spirit.
I receive God's mercy and grace to forgive
all those who sin against me.
Amen.**

He said to His disciples, "It is inevitable that stumbling blocks come, but woe to him through whom they come! It would be better for him if a millstone were hung around his neck and he were thrown into the sea, than that he would cause one of these little ones to stumble." (Luke 17:1-2)

Write down what God speaks to you through the Scriptures and by the Holy Spirit:

_____

_____

_____

_____

_____

_____

_____

Write down a prayer of advance praise for what God is and will be doing in and through you as you release and receive.

_____

_____

_____

_____

_____

_____

_____

_____

Memorize the above Scripture passage. Write the declaration and Scripture passage on a card to carry on your person or put it into your smart phone as a note or voice message. Read or hear it and declare it once an hour throughout the day. *Meditate on God's Truth this way day and night.*

Day 8

Release Self-Condemnation – Receive Acceptance

Declare this based on Romans:

**In the name of Jesus Christ,
I release all self-condemnation and insecurity within me.
I receive God's acceptance, affirmation,
and love for me in Christ.
Amen.**

Therefore there is now no condemnation for those who are in Christ Jesus. For the law of the Spirit of life in Christ Jesus has set you free from the law of sin and of death. (Romans 8:1-2)

Write down what God speaks to you through the Scriptures and by the Holy Spirit:

_____

_____

_____

_____

_____

_____

_____

_____

Write down a prayer of advance praise for what God is and will be doing in and through you as you release and receive.

_____

_____

_____

_____

_____

_____

_____

Memorize the above Scripture passage. Write the declaration and Scripture passage on a card to carry on your person or put it into your smart phone as a note or voice message. Read or hear it and declare it once an hour throughout the day. *Meditate on God's Truth this way day and night.*

Day 9

Release Insecurity – Receive Confidence

Declare this based on 1 John 3:

**In the Name of Jesus Christ,
I release all insecurity.
I receive the confident power to keep
His commandments, to believe on Your Name,
And to love God, others, and myself.
Amen.**

Beloved, if our heart does not condemn us, we have confidence before God; and whatever we ask we receive from Him, because we keep His commandments and do the things that are pleasing in His sight. This is His commandment, that we believe in the name of His Son Jesus Christ, and love one another, just as He commanded us. (1 John 3:21-23)

Write down what God speaks to you through the Scriptures and by the Holy Spirit:

_____

_____

_____

_____

_____

_____

Write down a prayer of advance praise for what God is and will be doing in and through you as you release and receive.

_____

_____

_____

_____

_____

_____

_____

_____

Memorize the above Scripture passage. Write the declaration and Scripture passage on a card to carry on your person or put it into your smart phone as a note or voice message. Read or hear it and declare it once an hour throughout the day. *Meditate on God's Truth this way day and night.*

Day 10

Release Selfish Pride – Receive Boldness

Declare this based on Hebrews 4:14-16.

**In the Name of the Lord Jesus Christ,
I release all selfish pride and timidity.
I receive boldness to come to the Throne of Grace.
I thank you, Jesus Christ, for being my
High Priest in the heavenlies.
Amen.**

Seeing then that we have a great High Priest who has passed through the heavens, Jesus the Son of God, let us hold fast our confession. For we do not have a High Priest who cannot sympathize with our weaknesses, but was in all points tempted as we are, yet without sin. Let us therefore come boldly to the throne of grace, that we may obtain mercy and find grace to help in time of need. (Hebrews 4:14-16)

Write down what God speaks to you through the Scriptures and by the Holy Spirit:

Write down a prayer of advance praise for what God is and will be doing in and through you as you release and receive.

_____

_____

_____

_____

_____

_____

_____

_____

Memorize the above Scripture passage. Write the declaration and Scripture passage on a card to carry on your person or put it into your smart phone as a note or voice message. Read or hear it and declare it once an hour throughout the day. *Meditate on God's Truth this way day and night.*

Day 11

Release Sowing to the Flesh – Receive Sowing to the Spirit

Declare this based on Galatians 6:

**In the Name of Jesus Christ,
I release sowing to the flesh.
I receive seed for sowing to the Spirit.
I thank you Lord for the bountiful harvest to come.
Amen.**

"Do not be deceived, God is not mocked; for whatever a man sows, that he will also reap. For he who sows to his flesh will of the flesh reap corruption, but he who sows to the Spirit will of the Spirit reap everlasting life. And let us not grow weary while doing good, for in due season we shall reap if we do not lose heart. Therefore, as we have opportunity, let us do good to all, especially to those who are of the household of faith" (Galatians 6:7-10 NKJV).

Write down what God speaks to you through the Scriptures and by the Holy Spirit:

_____

_____

_____

_____

_____

_____

Write down a prayer of advance praise for what God is and will be doing in and through you as you release and receive.

_____

_____

_____

_____

_____

_____

_____

_____

Memorize the above Scripture passage. Write the declaration and Scripture passage on a card to carry on your person or put it into your smart phone as a note or voice message. Read or hear it and declare it once an hour throughout the day. *Meditate on God's Truth this way day and night.*

Day 12

Release the Works of the Flesh –
Receive the Fruit of the Spirit

Declare this based on Galatians 5:

**In the Name of Jesus Christ,
I release the works of the flesh.
I receive the fruit of the Spirit.
Amen.**

The fruit of the Spirit is love, joy, peace, longsuffering, kindness, goodness, faithfulness, gentleness, self-control. (Galatians 5:22-23)

Write down what God speaks to you through the Scriptures and by the Holy Spirit:

_____

_____

_____

_____

_____

_____

_____

Write down a prayer of advance praise for what God is and will be doing in and through you as you release and receive.

_____

_____

_____

_____

_____

_____

_____

_____

Memorize the above Scripture passage. Write the declaration and Scripture passage on a card to carry on your person or put it into your smart phone as a note or voice message. Read or hear it and declare it once an hour throughout the day. *Meditate on God's Truth this way day and night.*

Day 13

Release Inner Turmoil – Receive Peaceful Rest

Declare this based on John 16:

**In the Name of Jesus Christ,
I release all inner turmoil, anxiety, and unrest.
I receive the peace and rest of God in Christ.
Amen.**

*These things I have spoken to you, so that in Me
you may have peace. In the world you have tribulation, but take courage; I have overcome the world.*
(John 16:33)

Write down what God speaks to you through the Scriptures
and by the Holy Spirit:

_____

_____

_____

_____

_____

_____

_____

_____

Write down a prayer of advance praise for what God is and will be doing in and through you as you release and receive.

_____

_____

_____

_____

_____

_____

_____

_____

Memorize the above Scripture passage. Write the declaration and Scripture passage on a card to carry on your person or put it into your smart phone as a note or voice message. Read or hear it and declare it once an hour throughout the day. *Meditate on God's Truth this way day and night.*

Day 14

Release Good Ideas – Receive God Ideas

Declare this based on Jeremiah 29:

**In the Name of Jesus Christ,
I release my plans and good ideas.
I receive God's plans and God's ideas.
Amen.**

*"... For I know the plans that I have for you," declares
the Lord, "plans for welfare and not for calamity
to give you a future and a hope." (Jeremiah 29:11)*

Write down what God speaks to you through the Scriptures
and by the Holy Spirit:

_____

_____

_____

_____

_____

_____

_____

_____

Write down a prayer of advance praise for what God is and will be doing in and through you as you release and receive.

_____

_____

_____

_____

_____

_____

_____

_____

Memorize the above Scripture passage. Write the declaration and Scripture passage on a card to carry on your person or put it into your smart phone as a note or voice message. Read or hear it and declare it once an hour throughout the day. *Meditate on God's Truth this way day and night.*

Day 15

Release Depression – Receive Joy

Declare this based on Philippians 4:

**In the Name of Jesus Christ,
I release all depression, despair, and defeat.
I receive joy, gentleness, and victory.
Amen.**

*Rejoice in the Lord always; again I will say, rejoice!
Let your gentle spirit be known to all men. The Lord
is near.* (Philippians 4:4)

Write down what God speaks to you through the Scriptures
and by the Holy Spirit:

_____

_____

_____

_____

_____

_____

_____

_____

_____

Write down a prayer of advance praise for what God is and will be doing in and through you as you release and receive.

_____

_____

_____

_____

_____

_____

_____

_____

Memorize the above Scripture passage. Write the declaration and Scripture passage on a card to carry on your person or put it into your smart phone as a note or voice message. Read or hear it and declare it once an hour throughout the day. *Meditate on God's Truth this way day and night.*

Day 16

Release Worry – Receive God's Peace

Declare this based on Philippians 4:

In the Name of Jesus Christ,
I release worry, anxiety, and fear.
I receive a grateful heart and the peace of God.
Amen.

Do not be anxious about anything, but in everything, by prayer and petition, with thanksgiving, present your requests to God. And the peace of God, which transcends all understanding, will guard your hearts and your minds in Christ Jesus. (Philippians 4:6-7 NIV)

Write down what God speaks to you through the Scriptures and by the Holy Spirit:

_____

_____

_____

_____

_____

_____

_____

Write down a prayer of advance praise for what God is and will be doing in and through you as you release and receive.

_____

_____

_____

_____

_____

_____

_____

_____

Memorize the above Scripture passage. Write the declaration and Scripture passage on a card to carry on your person or put it into your smart phone as a note or voice message. Read or hear it and declare it once an hour throughout the day. *Meditate on God's Truth this way day and night.*

DAY 17

Release Wicked Associates – Receive Godly Friends

Declare this based on Psalm 1:

**In the Name of Jesus Christ,
I release those around me who are
wicked, mockers, and scoffers.
I receive those who are godly, righteous, and holy.
Amen.**

*How blessed I am when I do not walk in the
counsel of the wicked,
Nor stand in the path of sinners,
Nor sit in the seat of scoffers!
But my delight is in the law of the Lord,
And in His law I meditate day and night.
I will be like a tree firmly planted by streams of water,
Which yields its fruit in its season
And its leaf does not wither;
And in whatever I do, I prosper.*
(Psalm 1 adapted)

Write down what God speaks to you through the Scriptures and by the Holy Spirit:

_____

_____

_____

_____

_____

Write down a prayer of advance praise for what God is and will be doing in and through you as you release and receive.

_____

_____

_____

_____

_____

_____

_____

_____

Memorize the above Scripture passage. Write the declaration and Scripture passage on a card to carry on your person or put it into your smart phone as a note or voice message. Read or hear it and declare it once an hour throughout the day. *Meditate on God's Truth this way day and night.*

Day 18

Release Unbelief – Receive Faith

Declare this based on Matthew 3 and Acts 2:

In the Name of Jesus Christ,
I repent and release past doubt and unbelief.
I receive forgiveness, grace, and the gift of the Holy Spirit.
Amen.

Repent for the Kingdom of heaven is at hand
(Matthew 3:2). After Pentecost and the powerful
baptism of the Holy Spirit, Peter proclaims, *Repent,*
and each of you be baptized in the name of Jesus
Christ for the forgiveness of your sins; and you will
receive the gift of the Holy Spirit (Acts 2:38).

Write down what God speaks to you through the Scriptures
and by the Holy Spirit:

_____

_____

_____

_____

_____

_____

_____

Write down a prayer of advance praise for what God is and will be doing in and through you as you release and receive.

_____

_____

_____

_____

_____

_____

_____

_____

Memorize the above Scripture passage. Write the declaration and Scripture passage on a card to carry on your person or put it into your smart phone as a note or voice message. Read or hear it and declare it once an hour throughout the day. *Meditate on God's Truth this way day and night.*

Day 19

Release Repentance – Receive Forgiveness

Declare this based on 2 Corinthians:

**In the Name of Jesus Christ,
I release all godly sorrow, tears, and grief.
I receive earnestness, eagerness to clear myself, and readiness to make restitution.
Amen.**

> *Godly sorrow brings repentance that leads to salvation and leaves no regret, but worldly sorrow brings death. See what this godly sorrow has produced in you: what earnestness, what eagerness to clear yourselves, what indignation, what alarm, what longing, what concern, what readiness to see justice done. At every point you have proved yourselves to be innocent in this matter.* (2 Corinthians 7:10-11 NIV)

Write down what God speaks to you through the Scriptures and by the Holy Spirit:

_____

_____

_____

_____

_____

_____

Write down a prayer of advance praise for what God is and will be doing in and through you as you release and receive.

_____

_____

_____

_____

_____

_____

_____

_____

Memorize the above Scripture passage. Write the declaration and Scripture passage on a card to carry on your person or put it into your smart phone as a note or voice message. Read or hear it and declare it once an hour throughout the day. *Meditate on God's Truth this way day and night.*

Day 20

Release Shame – Receive Righteousness

Declare this based on Romans 1:

**In the Name of Jesus Christ,
I release all shame and powerlessness.
I receive the faith of God and His Righteousness in
Christ Jesus.
Amen.**

*For I am not ashamed of the gospel, for it is the
power of God for salvation to everyone who believes,
to the Jew first and also to the Greek. For in it the
righteousness of God is revealed from faith to faith;
as it is written, "BUT THE RIGHTEOUS man SHALL
LIVE BY FAITH.* (Romans 1:16-17).

Write down what God speaks to you through the Scriptures
and by the Holy Spirit:

_____

_____

_____

_____

_____

_____

_____

Write down a prayer of advance praise for what God is and will be doing in and through you as you release and receive.

_____

_____

_____

_____

_____

_____

_____

_____

Memorize the above Scripture passage. Write the declaration and Scripture passage on a card to carry on your person or put it into your smart phone as a note or voice message. Read or hear it and declare it once an hour throughout the day. *Meditate on God's Truth this way day and night.*

Day 21

Release Foolishness – Receive Wisdom

Declare this based on Proverbs 9:

**In the Name of Jesus Christ,
I release foolishness and the wisdom of this world.
I receive wisdom, knowledge, and
understanding from the Holy One.
Amen.**

The fear of the Lord is the beginning of wisdom, And the knowledge of the Holy One is understanding. For by me your days will be multiplied, And years of life will be added to you. If you are wise, you are wise for yourself, And if you scoff, you alone will bear it. (Proverbs 9:10-12)

Write down what God speaks to you through the Scriptures and by the Holy Spirit:

_____

_____

_____

_____

_____

_____

_____

Write down a prayer of advance praise for what God is and will be doing in and through you as you release and receive.

_____

_____

_____

_____

_____

_____

_____

_____

Memorize the above Scripture passage. Write the declaration and Scripture passage on a card to carry on your person or put it into your smart phone as a note or voice message. Read or hear it and declare it once an hour throughout the day. *Meditate on God's Truth this way day and night.*

Day 22

Release Strongholds – Receive Sanctification

Declare this based on 1 Thessalonians 5:

In the Name of Jesus Christ,
I release unsanctified flesh and strongholds.
I receive sanctification in the
Holy Spirit in my body, soul, and spirit.
Amen.

Now may the God of peace Himself sanctify you entirely; and may your spirit and soul and body be preserved complete, without blame at the coming of our Lord Jesus Christ. Faithful is He who calls you, and He also will bring it to pass. (1 Thessalonians 5:23-24)

Write down what God speaks to you through the Scriptures and by the Holy Spirit:

_____

_____

_____

_____

_____

_____

_____

Write down a prayer of advance praise for what God is and will be doing in and through you as you release and receive.

_____

_____

_____

_____

_____

_____

_____

_____

Memorize the above Scripture passage. Write the declaration and Scripture passage on a card to carry on your person or put it into your smart phone as a note or voice message. Read or hear it and declare it once an hour throughout the day. *Meditate on God's Truth this way day and night.*

Day 23

Release Ugly Thoughts – Receive Lovely Thoughts

Declare this based on Philippians 4:

**In the Name of Jesus Christ,
I release every ungodly, ugly thought.
I receive thoughts that are true, godly, and lovely.
Amen.**

Finally, brethren, whatever is true, whatever is honorable, whatever is right, whatever is pure, whatever is lovely, whatever is of good repute, if there is any excellence and if anything worthy of praise, dwell on these things. The things you have learned and received and heard and seen in me, practice these things, and the God of peace will be with you (Philippians 4:8-9).

Write down what God speaks to you through the Scriptures and by the Holy Spirit:

_____

_____

_____

_____

_____

_____

_____

Write down a prayer of advance praise for what God is and will be doing in and through you as you release and receive.

_____

_____

_____

_____

_____

_____

_____

_____

Memorize the above Scripture passage. Write the declaration and Scripture passage on a card to carry on your person or put it into your smart phone as a note or voice message. Read or hear it and declare it once an hour throughout the day. *Meditate on God's Truth this way day and night.*

Day 24

Release Selfishness – Receive Glory

Declare this based on John 3:

**In the Name of Jesus Christ,
I release anything in me that is self-centered.
I receive ever-increasing glory from the Lord.
Amen.**

But we all, with unveiled face, beholding as in a mirror the glory of the Lord, are being transformed into the same image from glory to glory, just as from the Lord, the Spirit. (2 Corinthians 3:18).

Write down what God speaks to you through the Scriptures and by the Holy Spirit:

_____

_____

_____

_____

_____

_____

_____

_____

Write down a prayer of advance praise for what God is and will be doing in and through you as you release and receive.

_____

_____

_____

_____

_____

_____

_____

_____

Memorize the above Scripture passage. Write the declaration and Scripture passage on a card to carry on your person or put it into your smart phone as a note or voice message. Read or hear it and declare it once an hour throughout the day. *Meditate on God's Truth this way day and night.*

Day 25

Release the Desire to Control – Receive Christ's Lordship

Declare this based on Philippians 4:

**In the Name of Jesus Christ,
I release my desire to control my life and the lives of others.
I receive His Lordship and strength.
Amen.**

I can do all things through Him who strengthens me
(Philippians 4:13)

Write down what God speaks to you through the Scriptures and by the Holy Spirit:

_____

_____

_____

_____

_____

_____

_____

_____

Write down a prayer of advance praise for what God is and will be doing in and through you as you release and receive.

_____

_____

_____

_____

_____

_____

_____

_____

Memorize the above Scripture passage. Write the declaration and Scripture passage on a card to carry on your person or put it into your smart phone as a note or voice message. Read or hear it and declare it once an hour throughout the day. *Meditate on God's Truth this way day and night.*

Day 26

Release Stinginess – Receive Generosity

Declare this based on 2 Corinthians 9:

**In the Name of Jesus Christ,
I release all selfishness, stinginess, and miserly behavior.
I receive grace, generosity, and the spirit of a cheerful giver.
Amen.**

> *Now this I say, he who sows sparingly will also reap sparingly, and he who sows bountifully will also reap bountifully. Each one must do just as he has purposed in his heart, not grudgingly or under compulsion, for God loves a cheerful giver. And God is able to make all grace abound to you, so that always having all sufficiency in everything, you may have an abundance for every good deed.* (2 Corinthians 9:6-8)

Write down what God speaks to you through the Scriptures and by the Holy Spirit:

_____

_____

_____

_____

_____

_____

_____

Write down a prayer of advance praise for what God is and will be doing in and through you as you release and receive.

_____

_____

_____

_____

_____

_____

_____

_____

Memorize the above Scripture passage. Write the declaration and Scripture passage on a card to carry on your person or put it into your smart phone as a note or voice message. Read or hear it and declare it once an hour throughout the day. *Meditate on God's Truth this way day and night.*

Day 27

Release a Critical Spirit – Receive a Merciful Spirit

Declare this based on Matthew 6:

**In the Name of Jesus Christ, I release my critical
and judgmental attitude toward others.
I receive an attitude of forgiveness and
mercy toward others.
Amen.**

*Our Father who is in heaven,
Hallowed be Your name.
Your kingdom come.
Your will be done,
On earth as it is in heaven.
Give us this day our daily bread.
And forgive us our debts, as we also have forgiven our debtors.
And do not lead us into temptation, but deliver us from evil.
[For Yours is the kingdom and the power and the glory
forever. Amen.]*
(Matthew 6:9-13)

Write down what God speaks to you through the Scriptures
and by the Holy Spirit

_____

_____

_____

_____

_____

Write down a prayer of advance praise for what God is and will be doing in and through you as you release and receive.

_____

_____

_____

_____

_____

_____

_____

_____

Memorize the above Scripture passage. Write the declaration and Scripture passage on a card to carry on your person or put it into your smart phone as a note or voice message. Read or hear it and declare it once an hour throughout the day. *Meditate on God's Truth this way day and night.*

Day 28

Release Being Ungrateful – Receive an Attitude of Gratitude

Declare this based on Psalm 71:

**In the Name of Jesus Christ,
I release an ungrateful and unthankful attitude.
I receive an attitude of advance and continual praise.
Amen.**

My lips will shout for joy when I sing praises to You; And my soul, which You have redeemed. (Psalm 71:23)

Write down what God speaks to you through the Scriptures and by the Holy Spirit:

_____

_____

_____

_____

_____

_____

_____

_____

Write down a prayer of advance praise for what God is and will be doing in and through you as you release and receive.

_____

_____

_____

_____

_____

_____

_____

_____

Memorize the above Scripture passage. Write the declaration and Scripture passage on a card to carry on your person or put it into your smart phone as a note or voice message. Read or hear it and declare it once an hour throughout the day. *Meditate on God's Truth this way day and night.*

Day 29

Release Feeling Unworthy – Receive the Image of Christ

Declare this based on Ephesians 2:

**In the Name of Jesus Christ,
I release feelings of unworthiness, insignificance, and inse-
curity. I receive the image and mind of Christ and
His preparation for doing good works
that glorify God the Father.
Amen.**

*For we are His workmanship, created in Christ Jesus
for good works, which God prepared beforehand so
that we would walk in them.* (Ephesians 2:10)

Write down what God speaks to you through the Scriptures
and by the Holy Spirit:

_____

_____

_____

_____

_____

_____

_____

_____

Write down a prayer of advance praise for what God is and will be doing in and through you as you release and receive.

_____

_____

_____

_____

_____

_____

_____

_____

Memorize the above Scripture passage. Write the declaration and Scripture passage on a card to carry on your person or put it into your smart phone as a note or voice message. Read or hear it and declare it once an hour throughout the day. *Meditate on God's Truth this way day and night.*

Day 30

Release Me Increasing – Receive Christ Increasing in Me

Declare this based on John 3:

**In the Name of Jesus Christ,
I release my fleshly desires as I decrease.
I receive Christ that He may increase.
Amen.**

He must increase, but I must decrease. (John 3:30)

Write down what God speaks to you through the Scriptures and by the Holy Spirit:

_____

_____

_____

_____

_____

_____

_____

_____

_____

Write down a prayer of advance praise for what God is and will be doing in and through you as you release and receive.

_____

_____

_____

_____

_____

_____

_____

Memorize the above Scripture passage. Write the declaration and Scripture passage on a card to carry on your person or put it into your smart phone as a note or voice message. Read or hear it and declare it once an hour throughout the day. *Meditate on God's Truth this way day and night.*

Endnotes

1   Brevere, John. *The Bait of Satan* Lake Mary, FL: Charisma House, 2014. Preface.

2   Farrar, Steve. *Finishing Strong* Colorado Springs, CO: Multnomah Books, 1995. p. 15.

3   Tozer, A.W. "Five Vows for Spiritual Power." Neve-family. com. Web.
http://www.neve-family.com/books/tozer/
FiveVows.html

4   "Top 22 Quotes By Tommy Tenney." AZ Quotes.com. Web.
http://www.azquotes.com/
author/18298-Tommy_Tenney

5   Ryle, J.C. "Christian Zeal." Biblebb.com. Web.
http://www.biblebb.com/files/ryle/zeal.htm

J onathan W. Allen, Sr., a native of Washington, D.C., is a Pastor,
Husband, Father, Grandfather, Entrepreneur and Author. He
was educated in both public and private institutions in the District
schools and leveraged athletic abilities to attend Elon College
(Burlington, NC) on scholarship. Pastor Allen is a graduate of
Nyack College and is currently pursuing his Master's degree in
Divinity from Virginia Union University.

An award-winning business-owner, Pastor Allen serves as
the President of Operations for FASTING Enterprises, founded
by his son, Jonathan Allen, Jr. He has been recognized by the U.S.
Small Business Administration as Prime Contractor of the Year,
Prince George's County, MD as Small Business of the Year, and
other organizations for his operational and marketplace success
leading several businesses. Through all of these accolades, his
faith in God and life of ministry, a call he accepted at a young age,
is what drives his pursuit of helping others and doing the work
he has been appointed to complete.

Jonathan recently added the title of "published author" to his list of attributes. His first work is a weekly devotional, "Not A Sermon; Just A Nugget," and shares 52 biblical principles that allow the reader to reflect on their life and walk with God.

Pastor Allen continues to preach the gospel and advance the Kingdom of God. Through Allen Ministries, co-founded with his mate and partner for life, Pastor Kimberly R. Allen (Pastor Kim), Pastor Allen continues to pursue his purpose and passion of working in the kingdom so that Souls will be Saved and Lives will Be Changed.

Jonathan and Kim Allen have been blessed to be married for over 31 years. They have two sons, a grandson and granddaughter. The Allens continue to contribute to the surrounding community as they live and work in Prince George's County, Maryland.